MW01052010

NO HEROES,
NO VILLAINS

New Perspectives on
Kent State and Jackson State

ROBERT M. O'NEIL

University of Cincinnati

❀❀❀

JOHN P. MORRIS

Arizona State University

❀❀❀

RAYMOND MACK

Northwestern University

NO
HEROES
NO
VILLAINS

Jossey-Bass Inc., Publishers
San Francisco · Washington · London · 1972

NO HEROES, NO VILLLAINS
New Perspectives on Kent State and Jackson State
by Robert M. O'Neil and Associates

The Jossey-Bass
Series in Higher Education

A report of a special committee of the
American Association of University Professors
to study the implications for
academic freedom and higher education
of the student deaths at
Kent State University and Jackson State College.
The views expressed are not presented
as those of the AAUP.

30755

PREFACE

Early in the academic year 1969–1970, the year that was to end in tragedy, a special faculty committee at Kent State University issued a report regarding several days of campus disruption the previous April. (The report is quoted at length on pp. 107–121.) That incident—little publicized in the national press at the time—resulted in the arrest of sixty students, the suspension or expulsion of many, and the banishment from the campus of Students for a Democratic Society. Reviewing these events in the relative calm of the autumn, the faculty committee expressed great relief that no blood was shed. The report commended the president and the administration "on the foresight and good sense they showed in their plans for avoiding that kind of violent overreaction that has stained other campuses." The irony of this commendation could scarcely have been perceived at the time. Seven months later, more blood would be shed at Kent State than on any other college campus in the United States. Students or young people have been killed by National Guardsmen in other college communities—Berkeley, Santa Barbara, Orangeburg, Lawrence, and Houston. But Kent State and Jackson State shocked the country.

Most Americans had never heard of Kent State University or knew only about the prowess of its wrestling teams. They assumed when they learned the tragic news of May 4, 1970, that violence had unexpectedly struck a placid academic enclave in the heartland of the nation. This impression of tranquility was largely a myth, but (in view of the lack of publicity about the events of the previous year) a wholly plausible one. Ten days later, when two black students were fatally wounded by police at Jackson State College, the myth moved south. The average citizen, knowing little more about Jackson than he knew about Kent, assumed an equally orderly and uncomplicated past.

The myth was as plausible as it was misleading. Kent and Jackson were not typical of protest- or violence-prone institutions. They were, indeed, the antitheses of the prototype university at which major student-police confrontations had occurred—Berkeley, Columbia, Cornell, Harvard, Madison, Urbana. Violence was most common at large universities and relatively low at the growing public four-year campuses of which Kent and Jackson seem typical. Disorder seemed to correlate closely with the selectivity of admissions policies (and therefore with the academic-intellectual distinction of student bodies). Socioeconomic levels also correlated with campus turbulence, supporting a generalization that lower-middle and working-class students were less active politically because they were upwardly mobile and rather traditional. On this basis, few campuses should have been quieter than those drawing the bulk of their students from the factory districts of Akron and Cleveland or the farm fields of rural Mississippi. Any study of the demographic data would therefore have identified both Kent and Jackson as most unlikely sites of major student-police confrontation.

But the record is to the contrary. Kent State, as we have already observed, was the scene of an incident in the spring of 1969 that aroused the interest of the House Internal Security Committee and led to two days of hearings. Jackson State was probably the first campus near which a young person was recently felled by a policeman's bullet with the fatal shooting of Benjamin Brown in the spring of 1967. The wonder is that his death attracted so little attention when later deaths at other campuses were widely noted in the press and made the subject of detailed investigations. And there was even more turbulence in Jackson's past. Each year since about 1967, there was what the college president on the day of the 1970 tragedy characterized as the "annual spring riot." These clashes between black students and the white citizens of Jackson were recurrent and occasionally violent.

Far more has been written about the six students who lost their lives at Kent and Jackson in May 1970 than about the roughly twenty-five thousand who survived. Yet the survivors—students, faculty and staff—determine the character of these institutions of higher learning. They make Kent and Jackson distinctive campuses, different from many other developing state-supported institutions. One can understand what happened only by perceiving Kent and Jackson as institutions, not merely as datelines in a time of crisis or transient points on a newsman's map.

Many studies have been made of the events of May 1970 at Kent State University and Jackson State College. This one differs from the others in several important respects. Most significantly, it is a study of an essentially academic and educational phenomenon and was conducted by members of the academic profession. The questions asked of participants and observers who were interviewed during site visits to both campuses reflect the academic perspective. *No Heroes, No Villains* concentrates upon the implications of the student deaths and subsequent events for the future of academic freedom, institutional autonomy, and democratic governance.

Included are a series of recommendations and suggestions to the faculties and administrators of institutions of higher learning. Despite the risks of extrapolating from a narrow data base, we think it appropriate—indeed essential—to share with colleagues across the country a sense of deep concern about the broad implications of

Preface

Kent State and Jackson State. This sense of need reflects partly the experience of the study itself. It also reflects, however, a gap in the discussion of Kent and Jackson—a failure in the abundance of published materials to draw attention to this aspect of the matter.

This study differs from others in a second important way. It presents the only systematic comparison of the two institutions, the only attempt to identify common factors in the two events or in the causes of the shootings. The central premise is that similarities between Kent State and Jackson State—largely unappreciated in other analyses—are far more revealing than the obvious differences. This work shows concern with the long chain of events that created the flammable conditions at each campus rather than with the spark or the conflagration; with institutional governance and the processes by which issues affecting the safety (and ultimately the lives) of its members are decided; with the possible relevance of the several statements of the American Association of University Professors (AAUP) on the governance of higher education and the extent to which these precepts were followed or departed from in the events of May 1970; and with what might have been done to avert those events.

This study was commissioned by the president and general secretary of the AAUP late in May 1970 because the interests of the professoriate seemed so directly implicated as to warrant a special inquiry. The committee originally consisted of John P. Morris of the College of Law at Arizona State University; Raymond Mack, then director of urban affairs at Northwestern University; Robert D. Cross, then president of Swarthmore College; and myself as chairman.

The initial mandate was to visit both institutions. Members spent two full days at Jackson State College on July 13 and 14, 1970. Two weeks later, on July 27 to 29, 1970, the group reconvened at Kent State University. At both campuses, the committee interviewed and talked informally with many members of the administration, faculty, student body, and surrounding community. (The numerous quotes in the text which are not specifically referenced spring from these interviews.) These discussions were all

xii

Preface

closed and in complete confidence. Lacking the subpoena powers that other investigative groups possessed, the committee felt such conditions essential to a candid and thorough understanding of the institutions and the events.

At the conclusion of our study, we have added a Related Documents section. Although some of these documents have been widely circulated, most will not be familiar to the reader; all will be of interest and are supportive of the text. Several are published here for the first time.

A few words of acknowledgment are in order. We wish to express our deep appreciation to the officers of the AAUP chapters at both Kent State and Jackson State who made arrangements for our campus visits and supplied much useful background and current information. We are also grateful to the presidents and many administrative officers who generously took time to talk to us about the tragic events on their respective campuses. We received the fullest cooperation from all persons we sought to reach at both institutions. In the preparation of the manuscript, we had invaluable help from Dorothy Snodgrass in Berkeley and Barbara Lambert and Marie Ludeke in Cincinnati. Vital research assistance was provided by Joan Wolff, and the material was carefully checked by Marcia Wilkoff. Professor Michael Geltner of Ohio State University read the entire manuscript and made many valuable suggestions for revision and improvement. Vice-president Frank T. Purdy of the University of Cincinnati gave wise counsel on several critical portions of the document. Members of the Washington AAUP office—notably, Associate Secretary William B. Woolf—helped in countless ways. From start to finish the aid and encouragement of Karen O'Neil were invaluable—directly and continuously for one member of the committee and indirectly for the others.

Cincinnati   ROBERT M. O'NEIL
September 1972

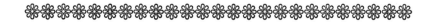

CONTENTS

Contents

NO HEROES,
NO VILLAINS

New Perspectives on
Kent State and Jackson State

There are no heroes
and few villains
in this unhappy chronicle.
There are people who made mistakes,
some grave.
There are other people
who lost their lives
as a result of those mistakes.
Yet no matter how exceptional
were the misfortunes of May 1970,
certain lessons of general value
emerge.

I

SETTING

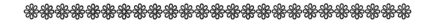

Let us begin where the press and the public began the search for answers in the months after the killings at Kent State and Jackson State. We reject at the start several superficially appealing, partially sound, beguilingly clear explanations that might simplify the inquiry. Because these theories have had popular currency, we offer them here, with tentative reactions.

(1) "Jackson State was simply a matter of race; southern white policemen hate blacks, particularly active young black demonstrators." Undoubtedly, much racial tension lies at the root of problems at Jackson and partly explains how policemen could shoot to kill. But this hypothesis misses more than it explains. The killing of the two students at Jackson was a most unusual event. Although blacks have been fatally wounded on college campuses before (notably at Orangeburg, South Carolina, in the spring of 1968) such

1

events do not occur with sufficient frequency to attribute the deaths to pervasive racial animosity. Even if one accepts the racial hypothesis, it is still necessary to know why, of the several hundred predominantly Negro colleges in communities patrolled by allegedly hostile white policemen, fatalities have occurred twice at or near this particular campus. Several questions demand answers that no simplistic theory can yield: How did the policemen get to the campus in the first place, and why were they able to load and fire their weapons without orders?

Moreover, to explain Jackson in this way says nothing about the parallel occurrence at Kent, where race was not a factor. Given the tensions that increasingly exist between long-haired activists and conservative policemen in white campus communities, it would be equally revealing to dismiss Kent by saying: It's just a matter of radical students and reactionary cops. No responsible member of the academic community would be satisfied with such a cavalier explanation of the Kent deaths. We can be no more satisfied with racial animosity as the single key to the Jackson tragedy, although race was undoubtedly a significant catalyst.

(2) "Kent State happened because inexperienced guardsmen were exhausted from several days of strike duty and then suddenly panicked." Even with regard to Kent, this hypothesis leaves open many critical issues: How did the guardsmen get to the campus in the first place? If they were exhausted when they arrived, why did the shooting not happen on the night of Saturday May 2 instead of the following Monday afternoon? Why have National Guard-student confrontations on many other campuses not resulted in bloodshed? How could panic in the middle of the campus have produced a fatal volley when experienced officers were presumably in command?

(3) "Kent and Jackson were just part of the post-Cambodia hysteria that swept the colleges in May 1970." Even the premise of this hypothesis is unsound; Kent occurred before the "hysteria" (if that is what it was) began. Moreover, the evidence now indicates that the Kent shooting itself, rather than the Cambodia invasion, triggered the massive student protest on campuses

across the country. The Jackson tragedy occurred after the crest of the wave had passed, although there was still much student concern about Southeast Asia. But the commitment to antiwar activity at Kent and Jackson never approached the levels at the politically active campuses—where no student deaths occurred.

(4) "The deaths of these students resulted from letting armed policemen and soldiers loose on a college campus in a time of extreme tension." Again, critical questions need to be answered: How did armed law-enforcement officers get onto the campus in the first place? Why were they left without supervision in the use of their weapons? Considering that campus police officers are armed at all times on a great many campuses, why have *their* guns inflicted no fatalities? And if confrontation was bound to lead to death, why not on campuses like Berkeley, Madison, Urbana, or Columbia, where students and police or guardsmen have faced each other angrily on many occasions?

We reject these simplistic explanations and others like them, although acceptance would make this analysis immeasurably easier. Yet, there is a grain of truth in each of these four hypotheses. Each to a degree describes the situation at Kent or Jackson. But real insight must come from other, more complex, often confusing data. We must try to understand both institutions—why they were typical and why they were atypical; how they were similar to one another and in what respects they were dissimilar—before we can begin to assess causes and assign responsibility. A thorough review of available information about Kent State and Jackson State seems essential in order to know whether the events of May 1970 could have been avoided and how.

Ultimately, certain phenomena remain unexplained. Numerous factors, trends, circumstances, personalities, and customs created a grave risk that something would happen at Kent about May 4 and at Jackson about May 14. The risk was not, however, the inevitable death of six students. Other investigative bodies have been unable to explain why, at a certain moment, Ohio National Guardsmen or Mississippi Highway Patrol and Jackson police officers opened fire. The President's Commission on Campus Unrest, in

3

its thorough and objective studies of both events, refuted several proffered explanations. It demonstrated, for example, that there probably was no sniper, that students were not advancing, that the officers were not in imminent peril. Yet the shooting took place. The ultimate psychological reality remains obscure and elusive to all who have studied these events.

Superficially, Kent State University and Jackson State College are dissimilar. They are geographically distant; one is four times the size of the other; one is situated in a small community, while the other is situated in a state capital; one has a local board of trustees, whereas the other is governed by a statewide board. The ranges of academic programs differ vastly. Perhaps most important, one institution is predominantly white, whereas the other is predominantly black. In the case of Jackson, "predominantly" is a euphemism; a federal survey conducted in October 1969 showed not a single white student registered there. Since that time, a few whites have enrolled as special students, but Jackson is still far less integrated than even predominantly white institutions in Mississippi. The same survey showed that at Kent black enrollment was about 4 per cent of the student body, which was average for a large public campus.

Below the surface, however, striking parallels appear. This chapter explores some of these parallels, especially as they help explain the events of May 1970. From this analysis emerges a pattern of remarkable similarities—a pattern which makes their pairing less fortuitous than is widely supposed.

First, both institutions experienced rapid expansion between 1960 and 1970. The 1960s brought general growth in higher education, especially in public higher education. But Kent State and Jackson State grew faster than other comparable institutions—so much faster, in fact, that they were atypical. The figures are striking: The faculty and student body at Jackson doubled between 1966 and 1970, which made it easily the fastest growing public institution in the state. Kent State enrollment roughly tripled during the 1960s, sometimes increasing about 15 per cent annually. These rates of expansion would be phenomenal even in states that experi-

4

enced major population growth during that decade—which Ohio and Mississippi did not.

The causes of this rapid growth also set Kent and Jackson apart from other public institutions. In a period when most states were forced to impose numerical ceilings and rigid restrictions on access to traditionally open public campuses, Ohio and a few other states retained an egalitarian concept of higher education. Although some diffusion of access and redistribution of students occurred (for instance, through the establishment of branch campuses, of which Kent State had eleven, and high attrition rates), the concept was essentially retained. Public institutions in Mississippi are theoretically more selective than in Ohio. In practice, however, Jackson entrance requirements for state residents (a high school C average or a satisfactory score on the ACT or SAT test) effectively keep the door open. Kent and Jackson expanded in more or less direct response to the rising demand for higher education, whereas public campuses in most other states were insulated in various ways—increasing selectivity, opening new junior or community colleges, and redirecting applicants away from oversubscribed campuses.

The consequences of this rapid growth are harder to assess than are its causes. We recognize here two mounting problems shared by Kent and Jackson. The first is internal, the second external. The student population on both campuses has grown much faster than the physical facilities. This growth has aggravated conditions, particularly at Jackson, which has long been desperately in need of new capital construction funds. Thus, in time of great tension, when the campus community is turned inward upon itself (by police cordon or town curfew, for example), the effects of overcrowding are felt in ways that would not afflict institutions experiencing moderate growth rates.

The relations between the campus and the surrounding community are also adversely affected by sharp rises in the student population. Large numbers of students seek off-campus housing when dormitory capacity is exceeded, a recurrent friction point, at least in Kent. In addition, the potential for abrasive contact between townspeople and the rapidly changing student generation

5

increases almost geometrically as the number of students grows arithmetically. The mounting tension between Jackson State students and white motorists along Lynch Street is therefore predictable, as is the rising hostility between Kent State students and downtown merchants and shoppers. The increased tension seems a wholly plausible result of the outward pressures of numerical growth upon a sort of demilitarized zone that had, until the 1960s, kept natural enemies at a safe distance.

There is more in the tension, however, than mere numbers. At the heart of community perception is the central mission of both institutions: to provide higher education and thus expand opportunities for youth of families for whom college is a new experience. The percentage of first-generation students on both campuses is high. Hence, the indirect effect of the academic experience is far greater than at institutions where higher education is a tradition. Working-class families whose children attend Kent State seem to regard the university more as a source of alienation than of opportunity—as the institution that takes their children away, changes their values, expands their horizons, and thus drastically realigns family and social relationships. Kent graduates will probably never join their fathers and uncles making tires in Akron, steel in Cleveland, or heavy machinery in Elyria. For the creation of such discontinuities in a traditional and stable community, the university is both praised and blamed. It is easy to understand the anxiety of working-class parents and neighbors, especially when radical politics, long hair, drugs, and loose sexual mores are associated with university life.

Jackson's role is perceived differently from Kent's by the community at large, though with comparable anxiety. The student body comes from nearby, but a large portion of the undergraduates come from the farms of central Mississippi and not from the city. As the student body grows, many Jackson whites, particularly those who have themselves been denied higher education, may understandably regard the college as the vehicle by which rural blacks are first brought to the city. Graduates will never go back to the fields that their ancestors farmed since slavery. Some go north or

6

west. Many feel that permanent emigration from the state drains off the best Jackson alumni. Those who do stay in Mississippi live in the cities and towns, many remaining in Jackson, where whites fear they may use their education and sophistication to incite trouble, raise demands, and arouse expectations in a long dormant but now awakened (and politically effective) black community. Thus Jackson State, much like Kent State, is hated and feared by many of its neighbors because it provides growing numbers of first-generation students the opportunities that justify its existence and support. Education is, after all, a potentially divisive force in society. And in communities where college has played a relatively minor role in life and work, the discontinuity can be quite profound.

The second major point of similarity is that both Jackson and Kent have essentially local student bodies but increasingly cosmopolitan faculties. About 90 per cent of the Kent students are residents of Ohio, most of them from northeast Ohio, particularly from the urban centers of Cleveland, Akron, and the surrounding towns. About two-thirds of the Jackson students come from within fifty miles of the campus. Few come from out of state. Thus, enrollment at both institutions is markedly local, as local as one would expect to find on any campus with dormitory facilities. (Clearly, though, neither Kent nor Jackson is in any sense a commuter college like the typical junior or community college or the campuses of the City University of New York.)

The local character of both student bodies also means that "radicals" or "agitators" are likely to be local people. It is neither accidental nor surprising, therefore, that the leaders of the expelled SDS chapter at Kent in the spring of 1969 were the son and daughter-in-law of the mayor of Akron. (Two of the four students killed on May 4 were nonresidents of the state. But, of the twenty or so Kent students indicted by the Portage County Grand Jury in October 1970, most gave permanent addresses in northeast Ohio.) Student leadership at Jackson, too, appears to be drawn almost entirely from the surrounding counties. Such radicals as there are seem to be native sons and daughters.

The origins of the faculties at both institutions are, however,

7

vastly different. Jackson professors, all black and mostly southern until the late 1960s, now include many whites, perhaps 25 per cent, in various disciplines. Several of those whites are native Jacksonians who have made a commitment of conscience at some risk to their community standing. The Jackson faculty is increasingly cosmopolitan, including many foreign-born and educated third-world persons, mainly from India, Pakistan, Southeast Asia, Africa, and the Caribbean. Among the native-born are a number with advanced degrees from distinguished institutions: a chairman of business enterprise holding one of the first Harvard doctorates in business administration, a distinguished critic of American letters with a Wisconsin Ph.D., and a young physicist with a Yale Ph.D. and a choice postdoctoral fellowship. The number of baccalaureates from Mississippi institutions is still high, but the percentage of advanced degrees from universities outside the South, many of eminence, is striking.

The Kent faculty, being substantially larger, is harder to characterize. The older core, a relatively homogeneous group, reflects the modest origins of the university as a teachers' college. But among the newer appointments, the diversity of degrees has markedly increased. In 1968, an eminent geographer, nearing retirement at the University of Chicago, joined the Kent faculty. He chose that campus because, over the years, he found so many Kent baccalaureates among his best graduate students. The percentage of faculty on the Kent roster with advanced degrees from Ohio universities remains high, partly, no doubt, because Ohio State and Case Western Reserve do claim eminence in many fields and partly because Kent is an increasingly important and attractive employer of new Ohio Ph.D's. The steady and rapid growth of the university was undoubtedly a significant weapon in the quest for academic talent that was, until 1969, a scarce commodity. In the 1960s, when Harvard, Yale, Michigan, and Berkeley Ph.D.s had to look outside the Ivy League and the Big Ten for starting positions, Kent seems to have held its own against such aggressive competitors as Northern and Southern Illinois, San Jose and San Diego State, Eastern Michigan, and North Texas.

No Heroes, No Villains

A third major point of similarity between Kent and Jackson is that both institutions are vulnerable to the pressures of a particularly hostile community. We have already spoken of one factor, rapid growth, that brought the campus community and the surrounding areas into collision more drastically at Kent and Jackson than in most other college communities. Let us now explore further this subject and point out the striking parallels in community relations between the two institutions. These parallels may help to explain the puzzling state of tension between the community and the student body—puzzling because the objects of citizen hostility were not residents of New York or California but, like the Akron mayor's son, who led the Kent SDS chapter in 1969, were the children of local citizens.

Several patterns appear in the relationship between campus and community in the United States. In the great cities, where the total population is large and diverse, even a big, unruly campus attracts relatively little attention. Even in the most turbulent times, the voters of New York City have not demanded reprisals against the students of Columbia or CCNY. Chicago aldermen are too preoccupied with pressing government business most of the time to care much what happens in Hyde Park or at Circle Campus. Agitation and even violence among Wayne or Temple University students is not likely to provoke harsh or repressive measures from local government.

In small towns, the college dominates the community and has relatively little to fear from local government. One cannot imagine the Hanover, Provo, Amherst, or Chapel Hill police as a grave threat to campus autonomy—not because the college or university necessarily runs local government, but because the campus is large enough to dominate life and public policy in a small community. Sometimes this relationship is reinforced by formal influence over the community—for instance, where the mayor is a member of the faculty (as in Ann Arbor) or where the student newspaper is the morning daily for the town (as in Ithaca).

Tensions are likely to be most serious in the intermediate situation: the typical community that neither swallows up nor is swal-

9

lowed by the campus. Eric Solomon wrote of Columbus that it was a community "of the wrong size and nature to assimilate . . . 'creeping universitism,' the quiet and steady arrival of men whose backgrounds were wide-ranging, whose views were varied, and whose commitments were to the general sophisticated intellectual community as well as to the local campus."

Kent and Jackson appear to be such communities. At Kent, the statistics describe the precarious balance: a campus population which is roughly equal to the population of the town but is growing much faster than the town and now threatens to overtake it, perhaps even to the extent of asserting political domination within the foreseeable future. (Town fathers, fearful of that prospect, apparently took steps to prevent it. The American Civil Liberties Union of Ohio filed a suit in the fall of 1970 alleging that local officials permitted Kent students to vote only if they could prove they never intended to leave the county.)

The Jackson situation is complex, for the faculty and student population constitute a small share of the growing capital area. But special factors make the college a potentially greater irritant than its modest numbers would warrant. Jackson State is the only state-supported institution within easy reach of the major metropolitan area and capital of the state. Except in medicine, Jackson whites who seek higher education but cannot pay the high tuition of small, private Millsaps College must travel to such remote places as Oxford, Starkville, Cleveland, Columbus, and Hattiesburg. None can commute to a four-year college. Jackson blacks, however, do have a choice of staying in the capital area or going to such all-black campuses as Alcorn and Mississippi Valley State. Moreover, Mississippi's level of support for all public higher education is so pathetically small that conflicts between individual black and white institutions, as well as between those two groups of campuses, are inevitable.

Thus, Jackson State College would be a potential target of hostility from the white community of the capital even if its students were completely tranquil. When disorder develops on the campus, any latent resentment at the choice location of this black college acquires a focus. And a sheer accident of geography (the location of the campus in relation to Lynch Street) has made turmoil at Jackson State the concern of the community in ways that only increase the irritation. These tensions are by no means new. Lynch Street has always carried white motorists past the Jackson campus. The expansion of the campus along the north side of Lynch Street during the 1960s and the growth of white suburban communities to the west have given added prominence to this traffic artery and have increased the possibility of conflict.

Tensions in Kent are also old. One university official, a Kent State graduate of the 1940s, recalls that townspeople even thirty years ago spoke angrily of the small teachers' college as "that monster on the hill." Some think that tension seriously worsened about 1967 when "the hippies began to arrive in Kent." As in most other communities, what probably happened is that about 1967 local youth began to let their hair grow and to affect an unorthodox style of dress.

The hostility prevalent in Kent and Jackson may differ only in degree from the temper of many small- and medium-sized college and university towns. Yet, these tensions are surprising for two reasons. We have already mentioned that the students are native sons and daughters. The campus is also a valuable resource for the community, a major source of employment, entertainment, culture, and consumer demand. Perhaps ambivalence is simply predictable under these conditions. But growth has rapidly multiplied the points of abrasion between academic and nonacademic communities, just at the time they are becoming more and more dissimilar through the cosmopolitanization of the faculties. The danger signs were obvious. But at both Kent and Jackson other warning signals existed.

A fourth major point of similarity between Kent and Jackson was that close ties existed between the governing board and the local daily newspaper. The chairman of the Kent State University Board of Trustees was also the publisher of the Kent *Record-Courier,* the principal source of news in the town, even though Kent is only eleven miles from Akron, home of the flagship paper of the powerful Knight chain, the *Akron Beacon-Journal,* which

11

devotes much space to Kent news. Similarly, one of the two Jackson members of the statewide Board of Trustees of Institutions of Higher Learning was Henry H. Hederman, a member of the family that owns the Jackson *Clarion-Ledger* and *News* and also television and radio stations in the Jackson area.

Such a close nexus between the major local media and the governing board is dangerous in the best of times. But with a crisis on campus, the threat to autonomy and objectivity is clear. Thus, it is especially significant that the *Record-Courier,* in the weeks after May 4, 1970, carried many letters from townspeople who were highly critical of students and supportive of the National Guard. It is clearly not fortuitous that the Jackson daily initially declined to print an editorial advertisement submitted by a faculty group criticizing the city police and the highway patrol for their role on the campus May 13 and 14, 1970.

The fifth point of similarity is the tense relations which existed between the student population and an adjacent nonstudent youth community. The parallels in this respect are less obvious. Corner boys, young nonstudents who frequent the bars and cafes on and near Lynch Street, have been a continuing problem to Jackson State. President John A. Peoples recalled the unsettling role of these bystanders even during his own student days and felt that they continued to complicate university-community relationships. Similarly, the bars along North Water Street in Kent draw not only students on Friday evenings but young people from a wide area, largely because several surrounding counties are dry. Such nonstudents were involved both in the downtown Kent disturbance of May 1, 1970, which led to the calling in of the Guard, and in the Jackson events of May 13.

The problem is not so much one of conflict between students and Jackson corner boys or Ohio farm youth. Rather, the campus and its administration have often been blamed for many transgressions of these hangers-on or bystanders as well as for the sins of their own students. A president cannot effectively disclaim such liability, but he has no power to keep these youthful troublemakers away from the campus environs. The imputation of vicarious responsi-

12

bility makes difficult not only the governance of the college, but also the development of cordial community relations.

The sixth point of similarity is that the relationships with law enforcement agencies failed to protect campus security or autonomy adequately. In terms of understanding and liaison with local government and law enforcement, both Kent and Jackson had probably gone further than many public colleges and universities. Although the emergency procedures and police-calling arrangements were deficient on paper, practical arrangements were more effective. Yet, through bad luck, poor timing, or human error, these arrangements did not function properly at the critical moment. Administrative officials at Kent had held monthly meetings with city officials, including police personnel, since late 1968 or early 1969. (Faculty and students apparently had not been involved.) From these discussions emerged an informal understanding that the campus was the primary concern of the university administration, and the town that of the mayor. Thus, city police (or state highway patrol) would come to campus only at the specific request of the vice-president for student affairs. It was widely supposed, too, that the National Guard would come only if the president asked the governor for help in that form.

In January 1970, Leroy Satrom took over Kent city hall. The monthly talks continued but without the developed background of understanding or accord. In the view of at least one university official, Mayor Satrom felt from the outset, as his predecessor had not, that "his responsibility extends to any disturbance on the campus as well as [to those] in the town." The former mayor had worked out a practical and successful antidote to trouble on North Water Street: He would call the six bars and ask them to serve free beer for the balance of the evening so as to keep people indoors and occupied. Satrom either did not know of this common-sense cure for unrest or rejected it on the night of May 1, 1970, and resorted immediately to harsher measures.

The liaison in Jackson also relied heavily upon informal understandings and personal contacts. Since taking office in 1967, Peoples had found the mayor and other Jackson officials generally cooperative. They respected the autonomy of the campus and, more important, they deferred to the president's judgment about the closing of Lynch Street. The delicate maneuver was accomplished on many occasions in this fashion: The president, after consulting at least with the dean of students, told the mayor or someone in his office that Lynch Street should be closed. Barricades were then set up at key intersections to keep traffic out of the campus area. Those barricades nearest the campus were manned by officers drawn from among the nineteen black Jackson policemen. White officers manned the farther ring of barricades and dealt with white motorists who had to be diverted from Lynch Street as they traveled home. The campus security force was then able to devote its entire energies to internal problems.

However, the whole liaison procedure broke down on May 14, 1970. Several unusual factors account for the lapse. First, through a curious irony, the police officer most experienced in handling civil disorders was out of the state attending a special seminar in riot control. Second, there was a critical break in communication about the status of Lynch Street on the night of May 14. Peoples felt uneasy during that day, and early in the evening called city hall to request that Lynch Street again be closed. Mayor Russell C. Davis insists the message never got through: "If those who were in a position to know the situation had requested me to close the street, I would have ordered the street closed." Since Davis had previously held Peoples a person "in a position to know the situation," probably communication critically broke down in Jackson city hall.

Later revelations explain how such a hiatus could have occurred. Two months after the shootings, a Hinds County grand jury explored the situation and in its report sharply criticized Davis. Davis, in turn, made a public statement placing much of the blame on the administration of the police department. (In May, Davis had stated on television his belief that no Jackson policeman fired his gun on the campus, a claim later proved to be based upon outright lies by several police officials.) In fact, it was later revealed that the mayor had tried to fire the chief of police a year earlier but had withdrawn his removal request "because it would have resulted in serious disruptions of the police department." But the breach continued to widen between Davis and a chief he declared "for more than ten years . . . had not really been in charge of the police department."

So, by May 1970, it was altogether plausible that Peoples' urgent request regarding Lynch Street was never conveyed from the police desk to the mayor's home but that instead the police made their own judgment about how to handle the campus situation. Given the absence of the ranking officer best trained in riot and demonstration control, the poor quality of that judgment becomes more understandable. Meanwhile, Peoples and his associates at the college, knowing little, if anything, of this conflict and confusion, reasonably assumed that the time-tested informal arrangements would bring barricades to Lynch Street instead of bullets.

The organization of the faculties of both institutions inadequately matched the needs of crisis. Faculties of colleges and universities, to the extent they are organized at all, typically reflect the needs of normal times rather than crisis periods. Kent State and Jackson State were not exceptional in this regard. The origins of faculty self-government at both campuses were, in fact, recent. The new Kent Faculty Senate, convened for the first time in the winter quarter of 1967, was completing its second full year at the time of the shootings. Its charter and by-laws were typical of the vast majority of senates which lack the long tradition and special powers of faculty governance: such as the senates at Berkeley and Minnesota. Shortly before the killings, Kent had appointed a faculty ombudsman—a significant innovation—to facilitate communication between faculty and administration and otherwise represent professional interests. The ombudsman, Harold Kitner, was to play a vital role as mediator and confidant during the troubled weeks of May and June 1970.

Despite this superficially adequate structure, Kent's faculty governance system revealed critical defects during the weekend of May 1–4, 1972. Several attempts through intermediaries to arrange meetings of faculty groups with President White were unsuccessful.

The president apparently felt that because the senate was the official faculty organ, and because meetings had been scheduled for Monday May 4 with both the executive committee and full senate, pursuit of informal channels on Sunday May 3 was inappropriate. Thus, there was apparently no vehicle for the presentation to the president of faculty opinion and concern about the condition of the campus. Only the secretary of the senate appears to have had effective access during the weekend to high administration officals. (There is one exception: The provost, the only member of the top administrative structure with a principally academic responsibility, was generally available to the ombudsman and others. He was, however, indisposed for part of the weekend, especially during the hours when the president's absence from the campus made definition of the chain of command critical.)

Finding themselves unable to reach the president, a group said to include twenty-three concerned professors prepared a statement on the afternoon of Sunday May 3.[1] This declaration deplored the invasion of Cambodia and the sending of National Guard contingents to Kent. It urged the removal of the Guard at once and "called upon our public authorities to use their high offices to bring about greater understanding of the issues involved in and contributing to the burning of the ROTC building . . . rather than to exploit this incident in a manner that can only inflame the public and increase the confusion among the members of the university community." Several hundred copies of the statement were distributed on Sunday afternoon.

There was evidently no official response to this anxious plea for the return of campus control to the academic community. Apparently, none of the proposed approaches was pursued. Several months later, the special Portage County Grand Jury investigating the May events on the Kent campus came across the statement and thought they had discovered evidence of faculty incitement on the eve of Monday's tragedy. The jury's report[2] concluded that even given the best of motives, their timing could not have been worse.

[1] The text of this statement is reprinted on pp. 122–123 in the Portage County Grand Jury report.
[2] Excerpted on pp. 122–128.

If the goal of the statement "was to further inflame an already tense stiuation, then it surely must have enjoyed a measure of success. In either case, their action exhibited an irresponsible act clearly not in the best interests of Kent State University."

The grand jury's condemnation is manifestly unfair. A small group of concerned faculty, seeing their campus rapidly becoming an armed camp under virtually martial law, tried unsuccessfully to talk with several members of the administration. Finding official channels blocked, they used the only means they knew to share their feelings with the rest of the university community. For their efforts they received the excoriation of an outside body—one wholly insensitive to campus conditions and realities. There is a special irony in the charge of irresponsibility. Among the signers of the statement were some who had served as faculty marshals under the most trying conditions during the burning of the ROTC building Saturday night. They knew the temper of the students. They also knew that disaster might befall the tense campus unless they could get their views before someone who had authority to take ameliorative steps.

The informal caucus of twenty-three professors was not the only faculty group seeking to convey its views during the crisis. The executive committee of the faculty senate met in emergency session on the afternoon of Sunday May 3, having learned that President White would probably be unavailable to them until the following day. (Even this group had more than the usual difficulty in convening. The chairman of the senate had said he would be out of town over the weekend. But the precise moment of his departure was uncertain. Hence, the vice chairman did not realize that he was the acting chief of the faculty until he went to the burning of the ROTC building on Saturday night and learned of the chairman's absence.) The executive committee drafted a brief statement, abhorring the damage and disorder on campus and in the community; urging all members of the university community to seek to return the campus to normal as quickly as possible; and pledging the senate to work to maintain the values of the university and community. The draftsmen felt that a public release of this brief statement would afford reassurance, at least by showing that the senate was still vigilant and functioning. Incredibly, the university's news bu-

17

reau declined to issue the statement, apparently believing it would inflame an already tense situation. The executive committee then tried to release the document on its own, with understandably limited effect.

The situation at Jackson differed from that at Kent in several aspects. First, the faculty senate was in its formative stages in the late spring of 1970. The initial meeting had been called for the week following the killings, but was cancelled when the campus was officially closed. The first task of the embryonic faculty executive committee was to draft and release a statement regretting the student deaths. Despite the absence of formal channels Jackson's smaller campus and the personality of the president ordinarily made the top leadership more accessible than it was at Kent. Early in the morning of the day of the shooting, President Peoples invited a group of students and corner boys into his house for an informal "gripe session." Apparently, no attempt was made to convene the new senate or executive committee later that day—either because there was not yet precedent for doing so or because it was widely supposed that the "annual spring riot" had run its course. By the time the senate was ready to gather, it was too late for any meaningful participation in campus decision-making.

Ultimately, therefore, the faculties of both institutions were unable to advise the president in time of crisis—in one case because channels of consultation had not yet been developed, in the other case because recently created channels had been blocked by circumstances. It is problematic, of course, whether greater faculty involvement could have averted the deaths on either campus. Nonetheless, a recognition of the vital stake of the faculty in such events makes participation essential, whatever the probable outcome.

The internal communication channels at both campuses failed to disseminate essential information. Internal communication systems, so critically needed in times of stress when rumors are rife, either did not exist or failed to function as they should have on both campuses. At Kent, the principal vehicle for internal communication seems to have been the *Daily Kent Stater*. Its columns ordinarily apprised students, faculty, and staff of late developments and sudden changes in policy. It would usually have furnished its readers a detailed account of the coming of the National Guard, the Guard's mission, and its authority. Ironically, however, the *Stater* did not publish on Mondays. Thus, the campus community remained largely in the dark about the state of siege from Friday morning until the following Tuesday—from a time before anything had happened until it was too late.

Various efforts were made by the administration to supplement this critical communication lacuna. Handbills and flyers were prepared over the weekend for distribution in the dorms and elsewhere. But it is hardly surprising that this informal, haphazard medium was not effective with a constituency accustomed (as are most campus audiences) to depending on the student daily. Moreover, there was a critical problem of credibility; many of the students and some of the faculty apparently lacked confidence in the administrators and students who signed the handbills as a result of the SDS incident in the spring of 1969. Yet, on the first weekend in May, there was not even a handbill clearly indicating the status or legality of the Monday noon rally, essentially because of lingering doubt in high places.

The communication channels at Jackson are harder to trace. The student newspaper, the *Blue and White Flash,* appeared only once a month and thus could hardly be expected to advise or warn of sudden developments. Much of the liberal Jackson community (both black and white) relied upon a new underground journal, the *Kudzu*—fittingly named for a plant indigeneous to the deep South which grows fast, runs far below the earth's surface, and is almost impossible to eradicate. But the *Kudzu* also appeared monthly. Thus, Jackson had to rely more than Kent upon word of mouth, meetings of departmental and dormitory groups, and posting of signs in the student union. The emergency student "gripe session" at the president's home in the early morning of May 14 illustrated the informality of communication patterns as well as the personal administrative style of Dr. Peoples.

The absence of regular and formal communication channels apparently made the Jackson State College community unusually

19

Robert M. O'Neil

vulnerable to rumors. Much of the tension that erupted on the evening of May 14 was attributed to a false report that police had killed Fayette, Mississippi, Mayor Charles Evers—the state's most prominent black public official—and his wife. The message spread rapidly by word of mouth, having apparently been spurred by several anonymous telephone calls to bars and cafes near the campus. There was no opportunity to check the rumor out and squelch it; it seemed sufficiently credible to many students so that further confrontation with white police may have seemed inevitable or even desirable. Thus, the often uneasy relations between black students and white policemen were further exacerbated by a malicious lie.

The emergency procedures of both institutions were ill suited to the events of May 1970. Almost every college or university has on paper a plan for dealing with emergencies—contingencies ranging from blizzards or epidemics to the death or incapacity of the president. Such policies are seldom reexamined, however, and tend to be automatically reprinted from one edition of the campus handbook to the next. So it was at Kent and Jackson; procedures, developed in a different era, were suddenly tested under extreme pressures and were, in certain respects, found wanting.

Kent affords an especially graphic example of how emergency planning can go awry when modern conditions have not been anticipated. The *Academic Policy Book* and the *Administrative Manual* outlined the procedures to be followed in the event of each of four types of emergencies: physical plant breakdown; inclement weather; student demonstrations; and national disaster.

The list was deficient in at least three respects, however. First, as one high administrative officer pointed out, no provision was made for *deciding* what kind of emergency was involved, so as to trigger the choice of procedure. General responsibility was placed in the president—a responsibility that might include this threshold decision. But in the president's absence—the situation which occurred on May 2 and 3—the rules faltered at the first fork in the road.

Second, critical responsibilities at Kent were delegated to

defunct and superseded offices—the emergency regulations having survived a major recasting of the administrative structure without revision. Moreover, the obsolescence of the rules created serious conflict between two seemingly applicable provisions in the *Administrative Manual*—a conflict which (we were informed during the visit to the campus in July 1970) "will have to be resolved soon."

Third, the critical matter of relations with Kent City, Portage County, and Ohio law-enforcement agencies received only peripheral treatment. The sole applicable statement provided that during student demonstrations: "Where necessary, the security officer is charged with seeking help from city police and sheriff and/or the state highway patrol."[3] The *Manual* does not mention the conditions under which such aid should be sought, the order in which the named agencies should be contacted, persons on the campus who should be consulted before or informed after such recourse, or the status of the campus police thereafter.

Jackson's emergency procedures seem superior in two respects. First, they had a more modern flavor and a more realistic view of campus disorder, suggesting a later revision. Second, they were printed in both the student handbook and the official faculty manual. Jackson's procedures also failed, however, to deal with many critical issues, including relations with the police, the role of the campus security force, the authority to call outside agencies and under what circumstances, and the responsibility to consult with campus officials. After detailing the conditions under which a rally or other gathering on the campus may violate Mississippi law, the regulation warned that a transgressor "shall be deemed guilty of trespass and subject to arrest."[4] The question of who arrests and when was left at large. (Jackson, like Kent, did, of course, have a network of informal, unpublished relations with local law enforcement. But here we are concerned solely with the sufficiency of the printed emergency procedures.)

It is not clear whether more detailed or current emergency

---

[3] *Kent State University Policy Book,* p. 99.
[4] *The Tiger: Jackson State College Handbook,* 1969, p. 35.

procedures would have improved the University's adaptation to the *emergency*. It seems unlikely that better policies would have kept either the Ohio National Guard or the Mississippi State Police off the campus. But sounder procedures might have improved the situation in certain respects—by making absolutely clear, for example, the locus of responsibility and by expediting communication between law-enforcement officers and university officials.

The lessons at both campuses seem painfully clear. Some of the breakdown in communication may have been the result of bad luck. But to the extent there was human fault, it rested almost wholly on local government rather than on campus administration. Yet, there is a disturbing lesson for the academic community as well: Informal arrangements with local government agencies are only as reliable as the men who make them—even when they are formalized on paper, which is seldom the case. If the key person is out of town or if someone forgets or if there is a sudden change in personnel, emergency procedures may break down. When that happens, the college president may simply not be notified. Perhaps the only safeguard against such contingencies is to rely upon informal arrangements with local officials no more than is absolutely necessary. At stake are nothing less than the security and the autonomy of the campus.

II

ANTECEDENTS

We have qualified one persistent myth: that Kent and Jackson were customarily placid institutions that suddenly erupted, like hidden volcanoes, in the spring of 1970. But there is a second myth that must be put to rest: that Kent and Jackson started a chain of violence in their respective states and drew gubernatorial wrath because they were the first members of the intrastate academic family to go astray. Although the facts are to the contrary in both states, the antecedents have not been much publicized. The popular tendency has been to isolate these two campuses for clinical analysis and neglect the relevant context.

Contrary to common belief, Kent and Jackson were not the first campuses in their states to explode. Let us review the true sequence of disorder in Ohio. On December 9, 1969, Governor James Rhodes mobilized the Ohio National Guard shortly after he learned

23

that the administration building at the University of Akron had been seized by student protesters. (A Kent official later observed that the Akron incident implied that National Guardsmen might be summoned hastily and without notice to the college president, because no warning had been given to Akron officials.)

Early in February 1970, there was a major demonstration at Ohio University in protest over increased student fees. Forty-seven students were arrested by state and local officers. On February 2, 1970, a bomb exploded outside the campus police station, doing substantial damage.

Shortly after spring vacation, during the second week of April 1970, violence came to Miami University in Oxford, Ohio. One hundred and seventy persons were arrested during a protest and occupation of an ROTC building; one hundred and fifty were students and they were all suspended. (A week later, the penalty was modified to permit the offenders to remain in school pending review of their cases.)

Finally, and most important, was the trouble at Ohio State. On the eve of the Kent shootings, several days of turbulent protest brought hundreds of National Guardsmen to the campus at Columbus. Several hundred persons, again mostly students, were arrested; eight students were wounded, and seventy-three injured. Tear gas and effective command of the Guard checked the formation of large groups of demonstrators and kept serious confrontation to a minimum. (One irony was not disclosed until several months later: Two of the leading "demonstrators," who had closed an open gate at a critical moment, were in fact agents provocateurs, state highway patrolmen in hippie disguises. A state official admitted the use of such officers during a student disciplinary hearing growing out of the Ohio State incident.)

Thus, by the first week in May 1970, violence on Ohio's state-supported campuses was an old story. Few institutions had been spared. Governor Rhodes had already acquired a reputation for prompt and firm response; he had called out the National Guard forty times during the preceding two years. In fact, Ohio's expenditure for National Guard duty is said to have exceeded the total for all other forty-nine states during 1968–1970. In fairness, this amount may have reflected partly the personnel limitations in the highway patrol, as well as the governor's determination to employ this particular mode of law enforcement. Moreover, when he got the news of the unrest at Kent, Rhodes was in the final hours of an ultimately unsuccessful struggle for political survival, seeking the Republican nomination for the United States Senate, an honor which went quietly to Robert A. Taft, Jr., on May 5, 1970.

The impulse to send the Guard to Kent in response to Mayor Leroy Satrom's request acquires plausibility from the convergence of these several factors: the mounting crescendo of disorder on Ohio campuses; the governor's increasing readiness to send the Guard to the site of any disturbance; and the imminence of his political showdown.

Politics may also have played a role in critical decisions at Jackson, especially the smouldering conflict between the mayor and the police chief. As in Ohio, the governor was critically involved. In a later speech, he acknowledged that he had mobilized the National Guard for possible duty and had sent several units of the Mississippi Highway Patrol to the campus on the night of May 13, 1970. And as in Ohio, an understanding of these decisions requires greater knowledge of previous events in the state system of higher education than is usually presented.

In Mississippi, as in Ohio, student protest was no longer novel by early May. About a year earlier, some fifty black students had been arrested following a protest at Delta State College. In the first week of February 1970, 894 black students were arrested on the campus of all-black Mississippi Valley State College at Itta Bena and taken to prison. Two weeks later, forty-one black students at the University of Mississippi were arrested on campus and taken to the same prison. Thus, within a little less than a year, about one thousand black students had been arrested in the course of campus protests in a state where student demonstrations, especially by blacks, were virtually unknown. When Jackson erupted on the night of May 13, no responsible official in the state could have been taken completely by surprise. Indeed, there was almost a feeling that Jackson would inevitably suffer the fate of her embattled sister institutions.

At Jackson State, there had been recurring clashes between motorists and students on Lynch Street as far back as current observers could recall. A particularly tense incident in 1964 apparently resulted from the serious injury of a Jackson student-pedestrian. A demonstration and several further injuries followed. There were the "annual spring riots," of which President Peoples at first thought the events of May 1970 were simply a recurrence. The most serious prior incident, in May 1967, brought death to one black youth and gunshot wounds to two others. The report of the Scranton Commission[1] recounts it:

> In 1967, Jackson City Police were pelted with rocks the evening of May 10 after chasing a student and stopping him on campus for an alleged traffic violation. A band of angry students and nonstudents roamed the Lynch Street area and set small fires, broke windows, looted stores, and threw rocks and concrete blocks at passing cars. Lynch Street was sealed off in the disturbance area. The next night, rocks were thrown at policemen who manned a barricade near a Lynch Street intersection several blocks from the campus. An officer received a serious cut on the neck after being hit by a thrown bottle. Reinforcements from the Jackson City Police and Mississippi Highway Safety Patrol were brought into the area. Some officers fired shotguns when a group of students and others advanced toward the barricade. One black youth, Benjamin Brown, was found dead in the street from buckshot wounds, and two students received birdshot wounds.

In addition, *The New York Times* reported at the time that after hundreds of students rioted, the governor ordered out the National Guard to take over the campus at the request of Jackson's mayor.

The background of disorder at Kent does not go back as far

[1] *Special Report of the President's Commission on Campus Unrest: The Killings at Jackson State*, 1970, p. J/5.

26

but is more complex. Two incidents during the academic year 1968–1969 are noteworthy. The first was a protest by the Black United Students and the campus SDS against the appearance on campus of recruiters for the Oakland, California police department. After a five hour sit-in, the administration announced plans for disciplinary action. Several hundred black students walked off the campus and demanded amnesty. Two days later, President White announced that no charges would be pressed. The black students returned and began pressing other grievances. Although an Institute of African-American Affairs was soon established on the campus, other complaints persisted. In the judgment of the Scranton Commission, "Blacks at Kent State remained less than content, and, after the sit in, relations between them and the administration were uneasy."

The major confrontation came in the spring of 1969. The campus SDS chapter had pressed four demands: abolition of ROTC on campus; removal of the controversial Liquid Crystals Institute (a research program partly supported by the Defense Department); removal of a state crime laboratory from the campus; and abolition of the degree program in law enforcement. On April 8, 1969, there was a confrontation at the administration building between campus police and SDS members seeking to post these demands on an office door. Several students were suspended, and the SDS charter was revoked.

Eight days later, a hearing was scheduled for two of the suspended students at the Music and Speech Building. Other students (who had demanded access to the tribunal, which the administration announced would be closed) got into a fist fight with fellow students, entered the building, and broke open a door. Campus police sealed the exits and called the Ohio Highway Patrol, which made fifty-eight arrests. The Scranton Commission notes: "Some students complained they were permitted to enter and then held inside for arrest."

An organization called the Concerned Citizens of the KSU Community (CCC) was soon formed to protest the handling of the events of April 8 and 16, the suspension of the demonstrators, and the forfeiture of the SDS charter without a hearing. A week later, the CCC was unsuccessful in a campus-wide referendum on these issues. Resentment was generated by the tactics employed by members of the administration and by student leaders opposed to the referendum, including the publication of a special issue of the *Kent Stater* (on a Monday, suggesting that such a special issue could have been prepared on Monday May 4, the day of the shootings). Particularly resented by CCC supporters was a front-page editorial headed: "Evidence Links SDS, 3-C," which many believed to be unwarranted and prejudicial guilt by association.

The impact of these events persisted. In October 1969, four SDS leaders, including the son of the mayor of Akron, were sentenced to six-month terms in the Portage County Jail. Those terms ended on April 29, 1970, two days before the events leading to the shootings.

A committee formed by the Kent State chapter of the American Association of University Professors undertook an exhaustive investigation of the events of the spring of 1969. This group interviewed many witnesses and examined a broad range of relevant documents. The report they issued in the fall of 1969[2] is described by the Scranton Commission as, in general, critical of the university administration's handling of the April incidents. This judgment oversimplifies, however, a complex document. Because of the importance of the report, we feel it appropriate to summarize the findings.

The report was divided into four main parts: the Music and Speech Building incident; the immediate or interim suspension policy; the formation and dissolution of the CCC (and response ot it); and the hearings of the student-faculty judiciary board. Major conclusions and recommendations were presented in each area.

With respect to the Music and Speech Building incident, the committee reached several pertinent conclusions. (1) Members of the SDS "engaged in irresponsible and criminal acts" in their attempts to disrupt the hearings. (2) The need to call in outside

[2] Excerpted on pp. 107–121.

police was not established beyond doubt; an emergency did not clearly exist, and possible alternatives for preserving order had not been exhausted. (3) "The decision to call for 'outside police' was taken without consultation with representatives of the faculty"—a consultation which, if followed, might have prevented such extraordinary measures. (4) Once called, the Ohio Highway Patrol "behaved, in a tense situation, not merely properly, but well."

On the matter of interim or immediate suspension, the committee reached essentially parallel conclusions: that the administration had acted within its legal authority in announcing a new suspension policy, but that the notice afforded the university community and the extent of consultation left much to be desired. (On the latter issue, "we are able to discern no way in which the university community was properly included in the evolution of the immediate suspension policy.")

The special committee concluded, with regard to the CCC episode, that debate on the group's status and its referendum was less than completely fair and impartial. Singled out for criticism was the special Monday April 21, 1969, issue of the *Kent Stater,* which the report found "tendentious" and lacking in journalistic responsibility, notably by "appearing to give authority to what was in fact unfounded rumor" (namely, the supposed ties between CCC and SDS).

Finally, however, both the special committee and the past AAUP chapter presidents expressed relief that the administration had handled these events so as to avoid "that brand of bitter, violent controversy given such unfavorable notice elsewhere." Prophetically, the report sensed that open conflict would not only have brought physical injury but through the media "would have focused the attention of the entire nation on KSU with consequences and dire reverberations in many quarters."

The report was submitted to the Kent campus community in September 1969. The report clearly identified several serious shortcomings in the then existing procedures: failure to consult adequately with faculty on security and disciplinary measures; insufficient notice of changes in disciplinary procedures; and imperfect adherence to due-process requirements in disciplinary hearings. The intervening months apparently brought no major changes in campus practice or policy to meet the committee's suggestions. The responsibility for this inaction rests only partly with the administration, of course. Blame must be shared with the faculty, namely, the senate and its Executive Committee, undoubtedly preoccupied with countless other tasks in a busy academic year. It is doubtful whether four lives would have been spared by effecting any of the suggested reforms. Yet, the campus might have been better prepared than it was for the events and the aftermath of May 4, 1970, had it listened more intently to the voice of the AAUP Special Committee. (Incredibly, by the summer of 1970, only one copy of the report could be readily located; that rare document was shared by the Scranton Commission and the national AAUP Committee.)

This review of the antecedents both at the state and at the campus levels leads to the following conclusions. By early May, violence had touched so many other state-supported campuses in Ohio and Mississippi that Kent and Jackson were almost anti-climactic. Yet, in both cases, there were special political circumstances making the use of excessive force dangerously probable. Albeit for different reasons, the governors in both states seem to have become hardened and determined to show their constituents that they would not tolerate more unruly students or further destruction of state property.

Both institutions had experienced severe disorder in previous years. Jackson had witnessed police gunshot wounds, and Kent, in the minds of many, had only narrowly avoided them. Having happened once, it could obviously happen again. Yet in neither case does there appear to have been major effort to reorganize the institution or its procedures to prevent a recurrence, even though, in the case of Kent, the way was partly marked by a careful faculty study.

Perhaps most important, officials in each state had developed a procedure for handling tense campus situations and making mass arrests without violence. In Mississippi, the critical experience was at Valley State, where 894 black students were arrested and taken to jail—probably the largest number of students ever arrested on a college campus in this country—with no blood shed, shots fired, or limbs endangered. The secret to the success of this operation was common knowledge around the state in the spring of 1970: The fifty-eight arresting officers were all black, drawn from campus and community police forces throughout the state. Their work was closely coordinated, carefully supervised with the help of the federal Law Enforcement Assistance Administration. Through a strange alliance between a black college administration, a segregationist white governor, and federal officials interested in improving Mississippi law enforcement, a sensitive and delicate task was skillfully and quickly executed. Thus, when it came to Jackson—superficially a far less demanding situation—there was ample precedent for avoiding precisely the kind of crude, uncoordinated, and undisciplined melee that occurred on Lynch Street the night of May 14, 1970.

Ohio also had pertinent experience from which to borrow. The use of the highway patrol to make the arrests at the Music and Speech Building a year before gave precedent. The situation was tense, the place of arrest relatively inaccessible, and the onlookers angry. Yet a carefully coordinated and swiftly executed sortie effected some sixty arrests without major incident, earning for the arresting officers one of the few kudos bestowed by the Kent State AAUP (Rudrum) Committee of Special Inquiry. In light of the arsenal of refined tools this experience afforded Ohio's governor, the use of such blunt weapons as National Guardsmen, exhausted from days of strike duty in Cleveland and Akron, seems as incredible as it is unpardonable.

Of course, there were reasons why the special black squad was not used at Jackson, nor the highway patrol at Kent. In a later section we review a number of parallel facts or occurrences on the two campuses during the critical days of May 1970.

On the afternoon of April 25, the Saturday prior to the Cambodia invasion and the weekend disturbances at Kent, the American Council on Education's Special Committee on Campus Tensions released its long-awaited report.[3] A major chapter sur-

[3] *Report of the Special Commission on Campus Tensions of the American Council on Education,* 1970.

31

30755

veyed "the college constituents, what's on their minds," with a section on "what's troubling the students?" Among the causes of student dissatisfaction and alienation were the standard grievances—international, national, local, and campus concerns—and some rather novel explanations. Into this matrix can be fitted most of the major campus disorders of the previous two or three years.

To what extent do the usual theories explain conditions of unrest preceding the fatal confrontations at Kent and Jackson? In all that has been written about these events, no detailed analysis has been made of the student feelings on either campus. Indeed, the tendency is to dismiss both incidents as spontaneous, not so much because there were no issues or irritants on either campus, but rather because of a lack of any visible causal link between those issues and the violence that erupted in May.

But at least one common event suggests parallel student concerns. Both campuses experienced attempts to set fire to wooden, highly flammable ROTC buildings—Kent on May 2, 1970, and Jackson eleven days later. The attempt was abortive at Jackson, where firefighters easily extinguished the flames. At Kent, the cutting of fire hoses, the presence of a much larger and angrier crowd, and the ineffectiveness of the campus police resulted in the total destruction of the home of one ROTC unit. Yet, there is little evidence that opposition to the training of reserve officers was a major catalyst on either campus, at least by the first week of May. (ROTC *had* been a major issue at Kent in 1969 when SDS was still active, but little had been heard about it after the organization's charter was revoked and its leaders jailed.)

Just before the fatal events, rallies were held on both campuses that did deal with identifiable student concerns. Jackson students gathered on the afternoon of May 7, 1970, to express concern about the Cambodia invasion and the Kent shootings, one of the very few predominantly Negro colleges in the country to experience significant antiwar activity that spring. But nothing occurring between May 7th and 13th imparted an inflammatory quality to issues discussed at that peaceful gathering. At Kent, it was, ironically, the black students who held the principal issue-oriented rally.

32

No Heroes, No Villains

The Black United Students (BUS) rallied on the afternoon of May 1, and there was anxiety about the outcome. But the meeting was peaceful, and fears of disorder were soon allayed—so much so that President White, earlier in the day uneasy about leaving Kent to attend the American College Testing Council meeting in Iowa, decided to depart soon after the BUS meeting adjourned.

One other smouldering issue at Jackson deserves at least passing mention. It is the incident of the bell, a controversy over the suitability of a proposed senior-class gift to the college. The administration and the Student Government Association had suggested earlier in the spring of 1970 that a campus bell, a collegiate symbol Jackson State somehow lacked, would be a fitting memento from the class of 1970. As word of the proposal spread, opposition mounted among junior classmen. The May 7, 1970, issue of an occasional underground student newspaper, *Voice of Blackness,* was devoted almost entirely to the bell controversy. The students had several objections. First, they argued that the money could be better spent on helping needy black families or setting up an emergency fund for students. Second, the middle name of the state's governor (John Bell Williams) made the particular object symbolically offensive. Third, student opinion had not been adequately reflected either in selection of a graduation speaker or in the choice of a bell as the gift. Handbills were printed and distributed on the campus under the heading "To Hell with the Bell!" Tensions developed, especially between seniors and lower classmen. An Associated Press reporter visiting the campus six months after the shooting interviewed students who recalled the issue. One student said of the shooting: "If it hadn't been for that silly bell, it might not have happened at all."

It is hard to assess the causal significance of this issue. Surely it is not the whole story; the report of the Scranton Commission omits any mention of the bell. Undoubtedly, many factors were operative at Jackson, creating an inflammable student sentiment under conditions that had produced a disturbance every year about the same time. The report of the Southern Regional Council cites as representative the explanation of one student: "It's a lot of

things; the war, Cambodia, the draft, the governor, Mississippi."
Another student placed special blame on the use of an armored
vehicle (nicknamed Thompson's tank) : "The sight of the damned
tank kind of got next to a lot of us. The tank is a big joke, but it
still makes us mad they have it. The only place they use it is on
Lynch Street." Thus, any effort to attribute the confrontation at
Jackson to a neatly defined set of student concerns is likely to
flounder badly.

The origins of the Kent clash are similarly murky. The weekend began, of course, with a disturbance that could as easily have
happened thirty years ago. Much like the "annual spring riot" at
Jackson on May 13, 1970, the North Water Street fracas on the
night of May 1, 1970, had many earmarks of an old-fashioned student frolic or binge just before final exams, almost predictable on
the first warm weekend of the spring. Indeed, the news from Kent
sounded strangely anachronistic on a Mayday when many other
campuses were embroiled in protest over the war or other serious
public issues—such as Yale's massive rally on the eve of the trial of
Bobby Seale and other Black Panthers for the murder of Alex
Rackley. Not until the National Guard arrived did readers in other
parts of the country first learn—on the morning of the shooting—
that the trouble at Kent had political dimensions.

Apart from an unfocused concern over the war, two themes
may explain both confrontations. One was student resentment over
public policy toward the campus—in Mississippi, the hostility of
the surrounding white community and the abysmal level of support
from a white legislature, in Ohio, hostility toward a town-dominated
local government perceived by many as oppressive toward the gown.
The other issue was an abiding bitterness between students and
law enforcement agencies. Tension at Kent mounted rapidly over
the weekend because most students (save those serving in the
Guard) had neither much contact with guardsmen nor any focused
resentment. Yet, by the morning of Monday May 4, and perhaps
even as early as Saturday night, there appears to have been widespread and deep hostility among Kent students. Not only the guardsmen but faculty members and others sympathetic to the students

have reported intense feelings. Tensions were exacerbated by several factors during the weekend: uncertainty about the authority and the orders of the guard; apparently excessive and occasionally painful use of bayonets to hustle students who were on the campus after the curfew hours; and a misunderstanding (the students thought it a double cross) over the effective hour of the Sunday night curfew. Finally, the presence of so many guardsmen on the campus for so long a period without adequate explanation undoubtedly contributed to mounting student hostility.

At Jackson, the tensions between students and police ran back deep into the history and culture of the state. Long after the limited integration of the Jackson city police force, the highway patrol remained 100 per cent white. Many students, their friends, and their families had experienced insulting or demeaning treatment at the hands of state police officers. The highway patrol bore the major blame for the unredressed shooting on the Jackson State campus of Benjamin Brown in 1967, the last time officers were officially there. Still under investigation in the spring of 1970 was a 1969 incident about which the patrol had been absolutely silent and not the least contrite, the beating of a black orderly and the arrest of two sympathetic white interns by a patrolman angered at the orderly's failure to bring in a drunk upon the officer's command. (The patrol eventually did transfer the officer and dropped the charges against the interns but took no other disciplinary action and offered no apology.) Shortly before the Jackson shooting, the highway patrol inspector in charge of the Jackson district testified in an unrelated proceeding that the patrol had no formal procedure for investigating charges of officer misconduct or for disciplining offenders within the force. Thus, grievances against the patrol that had smouldered for years always went unrequited. It was hardly surprising that the appearance on the Jackson campus of a highway patrol contingent two nights in succession created extraordinary tensions and hostilities among the students.

35

III

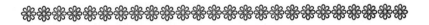

EVENTS

I t would be pointless for us to duplicate the work of other investigations by recounting in detail the events of May 1–4, 1970, and May 13–14, 1970. Those not familiar with these details may refer to the minute-by-minute account on pp. 99–106 as set forth by the Scranton Commission. Instead, we have decided simply to offer observations about those events. We have done so on a selective basis, applying two criteria: first, the special concerns of the academic profession and second, evidence of similar or common elements between the two institutions.

In both Mississippi and Ohio, the governors called out a law enforcement agency, gave initial orders, and then left that agency without adequate direction. The parallels are striking. On the night of May 13, Governor Williams gave detailed directions to the highway patrol to maintain or restore order on the Jackson State campus after disorder first broke out. Later that evening, he also mobilized the National Guard on a standby basis in case state and city police could not handle the situation. Yet, there is no indication that during the day or evening of the 14th the governor gave any further instructions or directions to either agency. Instead, it clearly appears that the highway patrol was on its own on the night of May 14. (The National Guard contingent apparently stood on the sidelines, awaiting further instructions from the mayor. We shall look more closely at the curious position of the Guard later.)

Much the same happened at Kent. Late on the afternoon of Saturday, May 2, the deployment of Guard contingents from Akron and Cleveland was authorized through the governor's office, at the urgent request of Mayor Satrom. On the morning of Sunday May 3, Governor Rhodes flew to Kent and gave the Guard commanders instructions on how to police the campus, even though they had ostensibly been called to maintain order in the town and not at the university. (Those university officials who knew anything about the coming of the Guard at first believed that their mandate included only civic and not collegiate matters.) Then, after waiting for a brief conference with President White upon the latter's return from Iowa, Rhodes left Kent to resume his Senate campaign. There appears to have been no further contact with the Guard either by the governor or by members of his staff. As with the Mississippi Highway Patrol, critical decisions were thenceforth to be made entirely by the battlefield commanders. Yet each governor, having dispatched to a troubled campus a heavily armed contingent which he alone had legal power to command, clearly retained ultimate responsibility for the conduct of the troops.

There was serious confusion and a critical lack of coordination among several law-enforcement agencies. In retrospect, it is impossible to tell who was ultimately in command of security measures at either campus. The most graphic evidence of confusion is the apparent absence in both instances of any formal order to fire weapons. It is not even clear which officer was authorized or empowered to give such an order.

The confusion at Jackson reached proportions that would

37

Robert M. O'Neil

seem comic but for the tragic outcome. At one time on the night
of Thursday May 14, just before the shooting, the ranking officers
of the three law-enforcement agencies on the scene (the Guard,
highway patrol, and city police) each had (according to the Scranton Commission[1]) "a different notion as to why police and highway
patrol units were moving up Lynch Street." Each had a distinct
view about the function of his own contingent and the responsibility
of the other two agencies. Moreover (the Scranton report again)
"in addition to the confusion about objectives, there were crucial
differences in procedure and training among the three law-enforcement agencies concerning the use of firearms."

Confusion and contradiction bedeviled Kent at two levels.
First, serious misunderstanding existed between the National Guard
and the campus administration over the nature of the Guard's authority and mandate under the governor's order. Much of the morning of Monday May 4 was devoted to disputes over permission for
the scheduled noon rally because of critical ambiguities in these
orders.

Second, serious failures of cooperation existed between the
Kent police and the campus security force. On the night of Friday
May 1, the town police followed a group to the main campus gate,
expecting the university security force to take over at that point.
The Scranton Commission reports: "The city police were annoyed
when Kent State University police officers did not arrive at the
gate to take over from there. City police did not know that students
were simultaneously congregating on campus and that the university
police chief, Donald L. Schwartzmiller, had decided to use his men
to guard campus buildings." The next night, the situation was reversed. During the burning of the ROTC building, the university
police sought aid from the town "but had been told that almost
the entire force had been mobilized and stationed to protect the

[1] *Special Report of the President's Commission on Campus
Unrest: The Killings at Jackson State,* 1970, p. J/21. References to
the Scranton report in the balance of the chapter are from the same
source.

38

downtown area." Schwartzmiller said later he received the impression that the city police were getting even with him for his failure to dispatch his men to Prentice Gate to disperse the crowd there on Friday night.

Against the background of previous interagency coordination in both states, such confusion and lack of cooperation seem inexcusable. At Mississippi Valley State College, the arrest of the nearly nine hundred black students had been effected without bloodshed because of careful planning and tight coordination among several levels of law enforcement. In Ohio also, policemen at different levels knew how to work together. Only the week before, reporters at Ohio State University quoted the commander of the National Guard contingent as saying that he was taking his orders from the ranking highway patrol officer on the campus. Indeed, much evidence indicates that the conflict at Columbus reached such proportions that fatal shots could first have been fired there, had the coordination not been so tight.

The presidents of both Kent and Jackson were excluded from the making of and even information about critical law-enforcement decisions. Clearly, neither president requested law-enforcement aid in the form in which it was deployed. Nor was either president consulted in the decision on whether to send officers to the campus, at what time, and in what number (much less with what equipment or under what orders), all matters of critical importance to the president and on which the president would normally be most expert.

Most seriously, neither president was formally notified that officers were being sent to his campus before they arrived. Of course, this statement must be qualified in several respects. At Jackson, it could be argued that officers were never really sent to the campus but only to patrol Lynch Street, which is city rather than college property. (All officers were apparently outside the campus limits at the time of the shooting.) Moreover, President Peoples undoubtedly suspected that officers might be sent on May 14th because they had been there on the 13th. But after his request that

Lynch Street again be closed, he reasonably expected black officers to be manning the barricades nearest the campus in accordance with the prior practice and understanding.

Qualification is important in the Kent case as well. President White was not notified of the coming of the Guard on Saturday, May 2, at least in part because he was in Iowa until early Sunday morning. During the day, several university representatives met downtown with the mayor and town police officials. At the last of these meetings, the critical decision was made to request the National Guard. University representatives—the vice president for financial affairs and the chief of security—were present at that time. But the Scranton Commission concluded that they left the meeting "under the impression that the National Guard was being requested for duty only in Kent, not on the Kent State campus." (The chief campus security officer testified that the highway patrol was asked to come to the campus earlier in the evening but declined on the grounds that there was no imminent danger to property. Later, when the ROTC building was in flames, the request was renewed, but then it was too late. Meanwhile, in default of the patrol, university officials decided they did need the Guard. By that time, notes the Scranton Commission, "unknown to them, the Guard was already enroute.")

The lack of consultation on the manner and the timing of sending police or guardsmen is probably more critical than the lack of formal notice. Also critical was the failure to arrange for the outside agencies to be briefed by campus security officers who knew the lay of the land. Even minimal consultation by the governor or a member of his staff with the president might have averted costly mistakes caused largely by the relative ignorance of officers sent to deal with an ominous and dangerous situation.

The law-enforcement agency given primary responsibility at each campus was unsuited to the special needs of the situation. Little doubt exists that the agency deployed was the wrong one for the task in both cases. The Mississippi Highway Patrol was especially abhorrent to the Jackson students and had little special training ing in riot or crowd control. The Jackson city police were potentially better prepared than was the highway patrol, but its potential was not fully utilized on this occasion because of the absence of the black officers and of the senior officer best trained in riot control. The Ohio National Guard was also unprepared for the particular hazard they faced at Kent. Though summoned several dozen times in recent years by Governor Rhodes, they had not received the extensive training in crowd or riot control that had been given guardsmen in other states.

Then there was the critical matter of weapons. Shortly before May 1970, the Mississippi Highway Patrol had inexplicably changed to a larger and more lethal size buckshot. Moreover, the Scranton Commission hearings uncovered the practice of permitting officers to carry their own personal weapons while on duty, a practice characterized by New Haven Police Chief James Ahern, a commission member, as "the most unusual regulation I've ever heard of."

The Ohio National Guard, meanwhile, came equipped with extremely powerful M-1 rifles, clearly inappropriate for crowd control. Whereas Guard units in many other states had been issued more fitting weapons (the Ohio Guard had at least once requested them to no avail), the contingents sent to Kent had nothing to shoot between tear-gas cannisters (which were so limited in effect that the students hurled them back at their source) and bullets that would carry two miles or pass through an eighteen-inch tree trunk at close range. Moreover, the Ohio Guard followed the highly unusual procedure of "locking and loading" before going into action with the result that each man in the field acquired complete autonomy in the matter of firing the highly lethal charge.

The irony thus revealed is cruel. In Ohio, the agency that had the equipment and the training to handle angry students was the state highway patrol as the Music and Speech Building incident at Kent in 1969 so well illustrated. In Mississippi, the National Guard was clearly the proper agency; unlike the Ohio Guard, they regularly carried unloaded weapons and could load only on orders of the commander and only as a desperate last resort. Unlike the Ohio Guard and any of the other Mississippi agencies, the weapons

41

they would load in such a contingency were special riot shotguns equipped with four rounds of birdshot and three of buckshot, to be fired in that order. The Mississippi Guard had, moreover (as the highway patrol had not), been trained and equipped to handle sniper fire. Yet as events turned out, it was the highway patrol in Mississippi and the National Guard in Ohio that went forth to do battle with the students. Worse choices could hardly be imagined.

Because of poor communication, misunderstanding, and simply bad luck, the appropriate agency was available but was not used. There has been no proof that either the Mississippi National Guard or the Ohio Highway Patrol was unavailable at the critical times. Indeed, the Ohio patrol was presumably fresh for action while the National Guard was exhausted from its six days of strike duty. The Mississippi National Guard had not been involved (as had the capitol district highway patrol) in the turbulent events of May 13. Why, then, was the proper agency not used?

In Jackson, the National Guard was mobilized (thirteen hundred strong) on the night of May 13, 1970, and it remained on alert through the next evening. The commanding general told the Scranton Commission that an informal agreement existed that civilian (city and state) officers would withdraw when the National Guard arrived. This withdrawal did not occur. The explanation for this lapse is uncertain. The Scranton Commission reports that, as state and city police moved up Lynch Street, the National Guard commander thought they were leaving the field to him in accordance with the prior agreement. However, "the police and patrol did not understand this to be their mission," and before there was any chance to confer or for the Guard to take independent action, the shooting took place. Apparently, then, the critical lack of coordination and of a single clearly recognized command prevented the use of the most appropriate agency.

Meanwhile, the abstention of the National Guard may have had another tragic consequence. Jackson's Mayor Davis apparently told the Hinds County Grand Jury something he did not tell the Scranton Commission because of the pendency of the state court proceedings. Davis testified that he had "delayed a decision on the use of [tear] gas until the Guard had moved into the area." Thus, although both the city and state contingents did have an apparently adequate supply of tear gas, they resorted instead to lethal weapons because of the hesitation of the Guard; the Guard, in turn, hesitated to move in because the police and patrol were not moving out as expected.

What happened in Ohio to the highway patrol? Even though the Kent State campus was clearly state property, the state police took the position that they would come only to make arrests. In the spring of 1969, the students were locked in the Music and Speech Building at the time officers were called in for the limited mission of arresting them and taking them away. Early on the evening of Saturday May 2, Kent State's police chief did call the highway patrol for assistance but was told that no aid could be furnished unless arrests were to be made. Later that night when the fire-bombing of the ROTC building provided a basis for arrests, the highway patrol was contacted again, but inexplicably did not respond until after the Guard was already in the vicinity. By that time, the issue was apparently moot and no further efforts were made to obtain state police help.

The irony is striking. At Kent, the highway patrol stayed back initially because they thought their services were not needed and later because the Guard had preempted the field. At Jackson, the Guard abstained at first because their intervention seemed unnecessary. Later when it was apparent that reinforcements would help, the highway patrol had preempted the field, or at least failed to withdraw according to plan. So the Guard remained in the wings, unaware that the mayor was apparently awaiting their coming as the signal to use the tear gas that might have spared two lives. In both cases, a curious twist of fate and a series of errors in understanding or communication denied a campus in trouble the steady hand of a competent agency. The hand that took over by default was inexperienced and unsteady.

The Kent and Jackson campus communities were taken by surprise. The president of each institution was neither consulted nor informed about the critical security decisions and other members

Robert M. O'Neil

of the two campus communities were even more in the dark. Jackson students may have expected that police would come to Lynch Street during disorder, but they must have assumed, as did their president, that only enough officers would be deployed initially to man the barricades and reroute traffic. The unannounced arrival of the hated "Thompson's tank" was also a major irritant. Kent students might have expected town or state police cars after the night of Friday May 1, but the unexpected sight of guardsmen equipped with heavy rifles and mounted bayonets, riding about the campus in jeeps, created the air of a military occupation.

There were other surprises. At each campus, a final order to disperse was given by a nonuniversity official but was not adequately conveyed to or understood by the students on the front lines. Needless to say, to those at a greater distance, the message was even less clear.

At neither campus was anyone prepared for the use of live ammunition. Many observers at both institutions—reporters, faculty, other persons, and students—have testified that when the shooting began, they assumed that the police had blanks in their guns, or at least were aiming far over the heads of the crowd. That officers would deliberately fire directly into a group of students on a hillside or into a girls' dormitory seemed incredible at the time to everyone except the officers themselves. The problem was not simply one of warning. Students know generally that soldiers and policemen carry guns and that the guns discharge bullets. Yet the whole history of relations between policemen and students on college campuses—often under circumstances far more trying than those at either Kent or Jackson—had furnished unwritten assurance that live ammunition would not be used, even if the provocation were intense. That assurance existed up to May 4, 1970. Only the naive would rely upon it thereafter.

The campus security forces were ineffectual both at Kent and Jackson. Like most colleges, these two institutions had small campus police forces, eleven men at Jackson (working three shifts); thirty-three at Kent. Little is known about the Jackson campus force, except that they appear to have played no restraining role

44

either upon the students and corner boys or upon the city police and highway patrol. It is unlikely that eleven men, even if all had been on duty that evening, could have played such a role, given the anger of the young people.

The recalcitrance of the campus officers at Kent is hard to explain. The entire force was on duty on the evening of Saturday May 2, the evening of the ROTC burning. Their station was only two hundred yards from the fire. Yet, they apparently did nothing to check the crowd. Several explanations are plausible. First, there were the tension and danger inherent in the situation. One faculty member sympathetic to and popular with liberal Kent students told the Scranton Commission: "I have never in my seventeen years of teaching seen a group of students as threatening or as arrogant or as bent on destruction as I saw and talked to that night." The official explanation given by the university's safety director was that a decision had been made not to subject the men to so tense and dangerous a situation, at least not without help from the Kent city police. But calls for help from downtown were unavailing. Eventually, after the fire reached conflagration level and the fire department had tried unsuccessfully to extinguish it, the campus police fired a few tear gas cannisters at the crowd and retreated.

Typically, campus security officers are not trained, equipped, or temperamentally suited for heavy riot duty. Under the conditions that prevailed at Kent on May 2 and Jackson on May 13 and 14, it seems unlikely that a handful of such officers could have brought order to a troubled campus. Yet, at critical moments, they could have given guidance to external law-enforcement commanders that might well have averted the shootings. For example, had the National Guard at Kent entrusted its most sensitive tasks to campus officers, enforcing the curfew on Saturday and Sunday evenings and dispersing the crowd on Monday, or at least worked closely with them, grave mistakes might have been avoided. At Jackson, where the officers were all black and had established a working rapport with students, the situation was different. The full contingent was on duty on the night of May 14th. They were used to check Alexander Hall and took posts at the doors of that dormitory.

But there was no occasion for them to check specifically for a sniper. The college's president reported that no charge of a sniper was made until the next day and then by a newspaper man. The problem at Jackson was different, therefore; yet the small size of the campus security force and the total lack of confidence in them by city and state policemen made them as ineffectual as the Kent campus officers.

At neither institution was the gravity of the stiuation appreciated until it was too late. On both campuses, relief that one night of disorder had passed without injury combined with a natural optimism to relax the guard of persons most responsible for security decisions. At Kent, meetings were scheduled throughout Saturday May 2, some on campus and some downtown. Plans were made early in the morning to keep students busy on campus that night in hopes of preventing a recurrence of the fracas of the previous day. Rock bands were engaged to perform continuously in the student union and the residence halls. But some observers felt the administration had misjudged the gravity of the situation. A *Los Angeles Times* reporter quoted one observer a week later as saying that "they did not seem to understand who they were dealing with. The students were desperate about the war, and the university offered them electric guitars."

Moreover, as the Scranton Commission noted, "the university had made no effort beforehand to prepare the students for the possibility that the Guard might come to the campus." When the Division of Student Affairs did prepare and distribute handbills, the text referred only to the Saturday night curfew in the town, but omitted reference to the more ominous 1:00 A.M. curfew for the campus. The leaflet also said that peaceful campus assemblies were permitted, a view that may have been technically correct but warranted explanation. After the governor's airport news conference on Sunday May 3, detailed leaflets were distributed stating that the Guard had assumed legal control of the campus and that all outdoor demonstrations and rallies, peaceful or otherwise, were prohibited by the state of emergency. (This judgment also required explanation.)

46

No Heroes, No Villains

The Jackson administration also underreacted to the situation after the first night of violence. On the morning of Thursday May 14, President Peoples issued a six-paragraph statement to the campus community, remarking that the latest of the "annual riots" had taken place the night before. He warned that there might be unpleasant consequences resulting from the incident. More specifically, he cautioned that six hundred National Guardsmen had been mobilized on standby duty in case of additional trouble at Jackson State or its environs. "My understanding," he added, "is that the guardsmen will be reluctant to use force; but if it is necessary to use force to protect life and property, it will be used decisively." Finally, the president told of his nocturnal gripe session with twenty students at his house and announced another one on the afternoon of Thursday May 14th for the same purpose: "Every opportunity," he affirmed, "is being presented to afford students a chance to air whatever grievances there may be."

Curiously, the president's statement made no mention of the more menacing presence the previous evening of city and state police. Only the National Guard drew attention, although the highway patrol had not been on the campus since the Ben Brown incident three years earlier. (Only the National Guard, President Peoples later stated, had officially communicated their intentions to come to campus if trouble resumed.) Perhaps the omission was attributable to the sense of calm and relief that President Peoples and his colleagues felt on May 14th. Classes and other activities went on as scheduled. No one seriously thought of cancelling an evening concert. Almost everyone assumed the crisis had passed, though even before trouble returned, Peoples was uneasy enough to feel that Lynch Street should again be closed as a precaution.

Hindsight in such cases invites unfair judgments. Looking back on the events of May 1970, it is easy to see that student feelings at both Kent and Jackson after the first night were like the fire that appears to have been extinguished but is in fact burning underground and unexpectedly surfaces at some distance from its point of origin. It is easy for armchair critics to say that extraordinary measures should have been taken by both administrations on

47

the second day because both campuses were in grave danger despite the surface calm. But those measures were not taken, nor would most college and university officials have acted differently as things stood in the spring of 1970.

The arrival of outside law-enforcement agencies displaced the normal decision-making processes and the internal authority of both institutions. It is almost idle to talk of faculty participation, student consultation, internal communication and the like when the effective management of the campus has passed to men like Inspector Lloyd Jones and General Sylvester Del Corso. By a series of steps, gradual at Kent, sudden at Jackson, campus constituencies lost the power to shape their destinies. President White, asked at noon on Sunday May 3 when he thought the Guard would leave, declined to speculate because "events have taken decisions out of the university hands." By perhaps ten o'clock on the evening of Thursday May 14, President Peoples could accurately have made the same statement.

It is easier to trace what happened at Kent than what happened at Jackson. Early on May 3, university and town officials drew up plans for a court injunction against further property damage on campus. Thus, in a sense, the administration voluntarily began the surrender of its autonomy by inviting judicial intervention in its affairs. (Two days later, without consulting anyone from the university, the same court ordered the campus closed indefinitely. The university apparently did not seek to have the decree dissolved or revised.) Matters remained relatively in the control of the administration until the Guard arrived late on Sunday May 3: the Guard whom most campus officials still believed were coming only to patrol the town. The troops set about at once to enforce the curfew and to herd students into residence halls, forcing some to spend the night in dorms other than their own. The university had one strategy for Saturday evening, and the Guard had another; the Guard's approach prevailed by force of arms after minimal consultation.

On Sunday morning, the governor came to Kent and legalized the de facto control of the campus which the Guard had assumed the night before. A hasty conference took place at the airport on whether to close the campus, a conference between the governor and the Portage County prosecuting attorney, without university participation, though followed by a brief meeting between the governor and President White. (The next afternoon, the county prosecutor obtained the injunction indefinitely closing the campus, affording its officers no notice until he had the decree safely in hand.) The governor's view prevailed, and the campus stayed open, but entirely on his terms. After he left, nobody knew what those terms were. Rhodes had declared the campus under a state of emergency, a characterization that may have been either descriptive or prescriptive. It was clear that some normal activities were forbidden, but disagreement persisted up until Monday noon about the scope of the prohibition. Ultimately, the National Guard commander gave the critical, and fatal, order to disperse the crowd on Monday because that suited his own impression of the governor's parting injunction. President White, asked what role he played in the final decision to break up the noon rally, has said simply: "none at all." Had the decision been in any degree his own, he insists that "from past history, all know that my response would have been affirmative to a rally."

It is more difficult at Jackson than at Kent to discover how vital decisions came to be made by policemen rather than by college officials. But there is little doubt the same displacement occurred. All the critical orders had been given, and the chain of events had been set in motion on the night of May 13th. The National Guard had been ordered to standby status near the campus; the highway patrol had been called to the campus by the governor; and the city police had been called out by the mayor. President Peoples played little if any part in these decisions, save perhaps in the original request to close Lynch Street. (On the night of May 14th, for reasons we have reviewed earlier, even that request was unavailing.) Even the Hinds County Grand Jury, not a predictably supportive body, concluded that the failure of city officials to heed the president's warning the second night gravely increased the risks. Although the precise relationship between the two key public officials and the campus is less clear at Jackson than at Kent, there is no doubt that

49

the governor, the mayor, and their deputies were in de facto control of the situation and that President Peoples was in fact as powerless as President White conceded himself to be. The responsible officials in both states probably had the legal authority to do precisely what they did. A state-supported college or university is state property and is also part of the city. There is no law in either Mississippi or Ohio creating academic enclaves where state or city police or National Guard may not enter. No statute or regulation requires the governor to seek the president's permission or even give notice before moving troops onto the campus. Doubt arises in the eleven states where the higher education governing board enjoys *constitutional* status. But even in California, where the board of regents is perhaps the proudest and most independent of all such bodies, there is no legal safeguard for the autonomy of any campus. Colleges are frail institutions and heavily dependent upon the goodwill and protection of public officials and agencies. When that goodwill sours, or when politically motivated individuals see partisan gain in invading the sanctity of the campus, no member of the academic community is safe. There is no place to hide.

Let us, in conclusion, ask ourselves: could it have been avoided? A definitive answer to this question is presumptuous. Any answer risks unfairness to those who made decisions at a critical moment. The benefits of hindsight are incalculable; yet we feel it is appropriate to our inquiry to speculate briefly about alternatives and contingencies. What we say here is, of course, prefaced by a realization that few municipal or university officials would in fact have done what in retrospect might have averted disaster.

Careful planning and coordination among law-enforcement agencies would surely have reduced the risks. At the time of Kent and Jackson, there were several striking examples of interagency cooperation and restraint. At Yale University, several hundred thousand persons gathered for the mass rally to express support for the Black Panthers on May 1, 1970. The National Guard had been called to the city. Connecticut state police were on the scene. But all forces were clearly under the command of New Haven Police Chief James Ahern, whose sensitive supervision of an extremely tense, delicate situation earned national recognition and esteem. Ahern worked closely with Yale University officials, who made elaborate provision for the housing and entertainment of visitors. There was a twenty-four hour telephone information service, where anyone could call to verify rumors or get answers to questions. The crowd eventually dispersed on Sunday May 3 without a single serious incident or injury. The situation would have been tense enough had the concern of the group been confined to the issue of racial injustice. But the invasion of Cambodia on the eve of the rally only raised the stakes and made the peaceful outcome the more remarkable.

Yale is not the only contemporaneous example of successful coordination. On the day of the Kent shooting, the National Guard was called to the University of Maryland, where they set up patrol. They departed on May 6 but returned when conditions flared up again on May 14 and remained for most of the month. The situation at Maryland was extremely tense because of student attempts to block traffic on a major artery (U. S. 1), which passes right by the College Park campus. Yet, not a single serious incident occurred during the whole month the Guard was on duty. The commanding general later attributed his success to several factors. His men observed strict discipline; they were repeatedly briefed on their orders to use no unnecessary force and to keep their weapons unloaded; they had just finished six months of active military training; and they were led by officers who had seen combat in the regular army. He concluded his testimony to a congressional investigating committee: [2] "The kids [in the National Guard] had their orders and they had leadership at every level. They followed orders."

There were, as we have suggested, relevant precedents, even in Ohio and Mississippi. The coordination of forces at Kent during the Music and Speech Building arrests, at Ohio State the last week of April, and particularly at the mass arrest of nine hundred students at Mississippi Valley State College suggests that Maryland and Connecticut have no monopoly on cooperative, carefully con-

[2] *Baltimore Sun,* June 12, 1970.

trolled use of law enforcement in sensitive situations. Somehow, the lessons were lost at Kent and Jackson, and tragedy followed.

As a special dimension of coordination, the matter of command also deserves mention. Clearly, at both Kent and Jackson, either a wrongful order to shoot was given (though there is no firm evidence of any order in either case) or the responsible officers simply lost control of their men while they were carrying loaded weapons in a highly explosive situation. Moreover, the officers responsible either did not know which of their men were likely to be most hostile to students under tense conditions, or did not care. Such leadership is bound to create the gravest risks, in sharp contrast to the kinds of law-enforcement supervision and coordination we have noted at other campuses where bloodshed was avoided.

Moreover, the use, by law-enforcement agencies, of equipment better suited to crowd control would have reduced the risks. We have examined several problems in this area: the wholly inappropriate M-1 rifles of the Ohio National Guard; the Mississippi Highway Patrol's unexplained change in ammunition; and its highly unusual policy permitting use on duty of personal weapons. We have also noted the failure of the Mississippi police to use the tear gas with which they were equipped, whereas the Ohio National Guard apparently ran out of gas at a critical moment or could not locate their reserve supplies. The remedies for these conditions are obvious. (Ironically, both the Ohio Highway Patrol and the Mississippi National Guard were properly equipped.)

Effective communication to student demonstrators of the order to disperse and of a warning that live ammunition might be used would surely have reduced the risks. As we have observed, an order to disperse was apparently delivered in both cases (albeit on dubious authority), but hardly anyone heard it or understood it. The use of communication media better designed to reach an angry, shouting, chanting crowd was surely called for.

Consultation with or at least notification of campus officials regarding crucial decisions about the security of the campus would have reduced the risks. Our survey suggests a critical failure to involve the college presidents in making initial decisions and in later reviewing the orders and instructions given to the commanding officers. There was also a failure to work with the campus police in either case, thus neglecting a valuable source of information about the campus and its people and a possible channel of understanding.

Communication within the campus of information that was available to the administration would have reduced the risks. We have noted deficiencies in the internal communication channels of both institutions. We have also remarked upon the failure of both administrations to keep the campus informed about the presence and prospect of law-enforcement intervention.

Emergency procedures better suited for modern campus crises and accurately reflecting working relations between campus and local government might have reduced the risks. Both institutions, as we have seen, did have emergency procedures on paper. But neither set of procedures adequately provided for a contingency clearly anticipated in practice—the need to call for outside law-enforcement assistance. Neither set of emergency procedures assured any consultation with or participation of other campus constituencies in the making of critical security decisions.

A more dramatic response to the first night of disorder, followed by continued emergency planning, might have reduced the risks. This factor is perhaps hardest to assess. With the benefit of hindsight, it is easy to see that the trouble was not over after one night of disorder. In fact, neither administration completely let down its guard. Yet, a combination of relief and optimism may have deterred the critical emergency planning that would have kept the campus in readiness for graver threats.

Had these and other things gone a bit differently, six lives might have been spared. Then again, policemen and guardsmen might somehow have taken matters into their own hands anyway. There is no guarantee that following different procedures would have averted bloodshed, although deaths and serious injuries were prevented in many other situations (New Haven, College Park, Itta Bena) where different procedures were used. The imprisonment of hundreds of students is hardly desirable. But it is preferable to death if a choice must be made.

IV

AFTERMATH

When the shooting had stopped, the dead and wounded had been removed, and the police and the Guard had withdrawn, both campuses became still. Within hours, each was closed and remained closed for several weeks. Each institution was, however, able to pull itself together for a regular summer session starting in June. By the fall of 1970, academic and other activities seemed to be back to normal; both campuses appeared to have recovered. Yet the scars left by the events of May were deep and indelible. In many respects, both life at Kent and Jackson and higher education in Ohio and Mississippi have been anything but normal since May 1970. The concern of this chapter is the quiet revolution that followed the gunfire. We begin with some general trends and changes common to both situations and then proceed to analyze separately the distinct sequelae in both states. To summarize at the outset, the two embattled campuses shared these experiences as a direct result of the events of May 1970: (a) Control of the campus and access to it immediately passed out of the hands of its own administration, faculty, and students. (b) Tensions between campus and community markedly increased. (c) Academic autonomy was threatened by a county grand jury report on the shooting. (d) Both institutions became keenly security conscious. (e) Conflicts and tension arose between state and local federal agencies. (f) Legal proceedings were brought against both Ohio and Mississippi and against responsible officials. (g) The legislatures moved to restrict disruptive student activities and prevent future violence.

The transfer of control at Jackson is easily described. On May 14th, after the shooting, at the President's request, the Board of Trustees for Institutions of Higher Learning ordered the campus closed for the rest of the spring term. The Alumni Association met as scheduled on May 23, but other normal activities were suspended until the start of the regular summer session on June 8, when the Board allowed the campus to reopen.

The aftermath at Kent is more complex. President White and his colleagues decided soon after the shooting that the campus should be closed immediately and that the students should be sent home for the term. At that moment, Portage County Prosecutor Ronald Kane was in Ravenna obtaining from the Court of Common Pleas an order to the same effect. When Kane returned to the campus, he met a university vice president who informed him of the closing. Kane promptly produced his own decree, asking confidently, "You're telling me?"

At first, it appeared that the court had simply reinforced the president's order. Gradually, however, critical differences emerged. Under the court's order, all authority to grant or deny access to the campus was vested in the Ohio National Guard so that at first even President White could not go to his office without the express permission of a military general. The terms of the injunction were later modified to shift the authority to other agencies. But control of passage through its own gates was not fully returned to the campus administration until the start of the summer session in the third week in June 1970.

An event which took place late in May suggests the scope of the court decree. The county prosecutor took advantage of the enforced vacation to search virtually all the dormitory rooms. Students had departed in great haste: some by reason of the closing, and others out of a sense of shock and grief at the shootings; few had carefully gathered their belongings. The search was carried on without notice to any of the residents, although their room contracts were still technically in force because the semester had not ended. When the prosecutor had gathered a handful of weapons (mostly jackknives, but also including a few guns) and some drug paraphernalia, he held for the press a display in the university gymnasium. No university official was invited to the briefing. The provost, who was the first excluded by the terms of the injunction, eventually obtained permission to attend and was allowed entrance by the Guard commander.

Thus, for some time after the shooting, the Kent campus remained more in a state of military siege than it had been before the shootings. The conditions of access were dictated entirely by the court, and the court was principally responsive to the prosecuting attorney who sought the injunction and requested its modification. The implications are frightening and by no means confined to Kent. During May 1970, in fact, civil judicial processes temporarily displaced internal campus governance at a number of institutions. While Kent was ordered closed, the University of Miami (which had suspended classes after May 4 in sympathy and support for Kent) was ordered by a state court to reopen. One campus of the City University of New York (Queens College) was ordered by a state trial court to provide designated hours of instruction in particular courses during the summer for students whose spring classes ended early as a result of "reconstitution." (Although the faculty members were presumably available and willing to provide the court-ordered instruction, students apparently never demanded that the decree be carried out.) New York University was ordered by a small-claims court to refund $277.60 to the parent of a student whose classes were suspended or altered by faculty senate vote the second week in May. (The judgment was later reversed by the Appellate Division of the New York Supreme Court, however.) Although none of these cases appears to have imposed final liability against the defendant institution of higher learning, the displacement of internal decision-making by litigation became, for a time, a national trend of alarming proportion. Should similar events recur in the future, such claims will almost certainly be taken back to court.

Tensions between campus and community increased after the events of May 1970. Relations between town and gown were, as we have observed, not particularly cordial in either Kent or Jackson before the shootings. Much evidence indicates that those relations worsened afterwards. Reporters returning to Kent found much community sentiment supporting the Guard and the prosecuting attorney. (This sentiment is exemplified by the report of the Portage County Grand Jury, of which we shall speak separately.) The Kent daily newspaper carried dozens of letters hostile to the university and few that were sympathetic. John Kifner, the *New York Times* reporter who had covered Kent during the spring, returned for the June commencement ceremony, the first activity permitted on campus since the closing. He found "resentment and fear among the solid middle-class citizens" of Kent. "There are few regrets expressed by townspeople over the deaths of the four students, and those few are usually prefaces to baffled outrage over the smashing of store windows, the burning of the army ROTC building, and the prevalence of long hair." President White admitted he was "a little surprised at the intensity and depth of the feeling" in the town.

There were some tangible manifestations of this hostility. On June 3, 1970, the Kent city council passed an ordinance prohibiting the burning or desecration of the United States or Ohio flag. (A student had burned an American flag on campus the day of the shooting and was arrested. Charges were dropped when the prosecution discovered Kent had no law making the act a crime. The new ordinance was designed to plug the gap.) Later in the summer, a measure placed on the ballot for the November election proposed the banning of 3.2 per cent beer sale in the city ward nearest the campus and the prohibition of live entertainment anywhere in the city by profit-making organizations. The aim of both measures, said the councilman sponsoring them, was to eliminate "undesirables" from the area.

In Jackson, the tension resulting from the May shootings was more a matter of racial conflict than age conflict. Conditions were unsettled even before the shooting. The city's eleven swimming pools had been closed for several years to circumvent a federal court order to integrate. A court challenge to the closing was finally rejected by the United States Supreme Court in June 1971. Since the beginning of 1970, the public school situation had been especially tense. Many white families had fled to private academies to avoid integrated classrooms. The city was under an injunction by the federal court of appeals to permit certain protest marches and demonstrations forbidden by its regulation. Much has been written and much more could be said about the state of race relations in Jackson at the time of the shooting. Suffice it to say here that the climate was tense in the capital, although probably better than in rural parts of the state.

The mayor's first response to the shootings was to appoint a biracial investigative commission, including two active young black attorneys. This conciliatory gesture may, however, have annoyed more citizens than it pleased. Whites were upset because so delicate and controversial a task was entrusted to a mixed body. Some blacks were displeased because the committee had a white majority to study a matter of primarily black interest. They were also upset because, without subpoena powers, it could not compel testimony of policemen who were bound to balk at such an inquiry. The Hinds County Grand Jury was later highly critical of the biracial commission and of the mayor's resort to its counsel. The mayor lashed back that "the formation of any biracial committee is abhorrent to those who seek refuge in the past. It may well be that this one act on my part is responsible for the vilification contained in the grand jury report." (His speech is quoted at length on pp. 159–165.)

Much more is known of the mood of Jackson's black community than of white sentiment after the events of May 1970. Testimony given to the Scranton Commission revealed a mixture of anger and despair among Mississippi Negroes, a mood probably deepened by the killing of the two young men. The Mississippi United Front, a black coalition formed originally to defend Head Start programs against official attacks, announced early in the summer the inauguration of an armed, black program for self-defense as a direct result of the Jackson State shootings. June Jordan, a Negro writer, talked during the summer with black leaders in Mississippi and reported her conclusions in a *New York Times* magazine article (Oct. 11, 1970). Although "black self-defense is not a new idea in this terror-stricken state," she observed, interest and determination had recently been spurred by the Jackson State and other fatalities. Characteristic of this new black feeling was the testimony of Dr. Aaron Shirley, prominent black Jackson physician and leader of the Mississippi United Front, to the Scranton Commission: "We don't plan to stand around and allow cops, under the guise of law and order, to shoot our kids for throwing rocks."

There are also, however, signs of a lessening of tension in Jackson, whether or not related to the shootings and college-community ties. Mayor Davis, later in 1970, attempted to appoint President Peoples to the influential city planning board. Although he was unsuccessful, he eventually did add a black to the city's school board. There are two other blacks in other appointed municipal agencies. Meanwhile, the Jackson Chamber of Commerce took the unprecedented step of inviting local blacks to participate in writing a comprehensive community-development plan. In place of the eleven swimming pools, which the federal courts held could legally be closed to avoid integration, the Chamber of Commerce recommended construction of ten new pools, some of which would apparently be integrated. Finally, and perhaps most important, the city council has at last been persuaded to close Lynch Street, thus removing a principal ingredient of confrontation.

It is also important that Jackson State was spared any disorder after the early summer of 1970. The year after the shootings passed somewhat less easily at Kent. The campus remained miraculously calm during the fall, despite pressures of which we shall speak momentarily. Early in 1971, however, there were sporadic incidents of disorder. On February 5, 1971, for example, the American flag in front of the Administration Building was hauled down and replaced by a Viet Cong flag, and a student was charged with flag desecration under the newly adopted municipal ordinance. In May 1971, a memorial period during the first week of May passed calmly, marred only by a twenty-four hour peaceful sit-in, which temporarily closed the new quarters of the ROTC. Later in the month, as the court trials of twenty-five students, indicted for their roles in the 1970 disturbances, got underway, there was disorder. Four days of disturbances in downtown Kent resulted in the arrest of eighty-seven persons, including fifty-one students, among them outgoing student-body president Craig Morgan. Charges of police abuses and violations of individual rights brought demands for an investigation; American Civil Liberties Union attorneys took extensive testimony from participants and observers. Yet, there were apparently no serious personal injuries, no major confrontations between students and law-enforcement officers, no damage to property either on the campus or downtown. Thus, as the year ended, a sense of relief pervaded that this badly scarred institution had been spared further wounds.

At both Jackson and Kent, academic autonomy was threatened by a county grand jury report on the shooting. It was natural enough in both states that grand juries should look into the fatal confrontations between the students and police. (Excerpts from these are quoted at length on pp. 122 ff and pp. 152 ff.) Six lay dead. Blame had to be assessed and criminal charges against the responsible law-enforcement officers considered. What was not predictable was the direction these inquiries took. Both grand jury reports found that a riot was in progress at the time of the shootings, that some law-enforcement officers believed they were firing in response to snipers (of which federal investigators found no reliable evidence in either case) and that Mississippi police and Ohio Guardsmen reasonably feared for their lives and thus should be exonerated of all criminal liability. The major blame for the confrontation in both cases was rested with the students and other demonstrators. At Kent, the university administration also drew criticism, and, in Jackson, the mayor shared some of the stigma.

The two grand jury reports are, however, differing documents. Each deserves separate attention. The Jackson grand jury was, on the whole, the more benign of the two. It included two blacks and at least one liberal white, thus providing at least some voice for the injured constituency. (The Kent grand jury, selected from voter lists, contained no students because few students appeared on those lists.) The Mississippi jury's sharp criticism of the students and strong support for the city and state police was partly tempered by deference to the judgment of President Peoples on the closing of Lynch Street—a judgment, which the grand jury felt, if properly communicated, might have averted disaster. This body reserved its harshest rebuke for Jackson's Mayor Davis, who had gone on television soon after the shooting to state that no city policeman had fired his gun. This claim was later proved false. Responsible police officials simply withheld the truth from several investigative groups, including the biracial commission on whom the mayor had relied. Not only had the mayor been deceived and in turn misled his constituents on this vital issue; the effect of his unfortunate misstatement was to place sole blame for the killings on the highway patrol and thus create tensions between city and state as well as within city hall.

After the mayor had discharged the police chief, he set about to redeem his own reputation. Among other steps, he asked the court to excise portions of the grand jury report that were most critical of him in his dispute with the police. His attorney pointed out to the court the highly unusual character of the report—essentially a gratuitous or advisory document reflecting the opinions of the grand jury, rather than a specific basis for indictments.

Unlike the sometimes temperate Jackson report, the Portage County Special Grand Jury showed little mercy to members of the Kent campus community. The conduct of the students was found reprehensible and criminal throughout the confrontation weekend. There was a "riot" Friday evening, the burning of the ROTC building on Saturday constituted a "riot," as did the demonstration over the curfew Sunday night. The Monday noon rally violated a valid order to disperse. Thus, the calling of the National Guard on Saturday evening was fully justified. The mayor had heard rumors that carloads of SDS members were on their way to Kent and reasonably feared for the safety of his town. On Monday, the guardsmen who fired at the students reasonably fired for their lives. There was evidence of sniper fire, tear gas supplies were exhausted and had proved ineffectual anyway. Apart from the rocks and other missiles thrown at them, the "language of the gutter" to which the guardsmen were subjected was highly provocative by itself. The report added two caveats: The commanding officers of the Guard showed poor judgment in handling the Monday dispersal because they placed their troops "in an untenable and dangerous position." Moreover, the use of the powerful M-1 rifle was unsuitable for crowd control, but no other equipment had been furnished. "Nonlethal weapons, more appropriate in connection with campus disorders," cautioned the report, "should be made available to the National Guard in the future."

The most troubling grand jury finding came toward the end. We have already considered the castigation of the "faculty twenty-three" for issuing their Sunday afternoon statement of concern, deemed by the jurors "an irresponsible act, clearly not in the best interests of Kent State University." The finger of blame pointed directly at "those persons who are charged with the administration of the university." They bore the "major responsibility" for the events of May 2, 3, and 4. Specifically, "the administration at Kent State University has fostered an attitude of overindulgence and permissiveness with its students and faculty to the extent that it can on longer regulate the activities of either and is particularly vulnerable to any pressure applied from radical elements within the student body or faculty." As evidence of laxity, the grand jury cited the small number of students expelled during 1970 (overlooking the swift and harsh reprisals of the previous year against the SDS), and the "overemphasis which it has placed and allowed to be placed on the right of dissent" (referring principally to recognition of student groups and the range of outside speakers permitted on the campus).

Finally, the grand jury showed its disdain for academic freedom: "A further example of what we consider an overemphasis on dissent can be found in the classrooms of some members of the university faculty. The faculty members to whom we refer teach nothing but the negative side of our institutions and government and refuse to acknowledge that any positive good has resulted during the growth of our nation. They devote their entire class periods to urging their students to openly oppose our institutions of government." Although the report acknowledged that such "negative" professors constituted only a small share of the total faculty, "this does not mean that their presence should be ignored."

The grand jury handed down twenty-five indictments, none against guardsmen or other law-enforcement officers, all against students, young nonstudents, and one member of the faculty. Professor Thomas Lough was indicted for the crime of "incitement," the details of which were not specified. Legal observers assumed that the charge reflected either an incident in Lough's sociology class a year earlier (the use, for discussion purposes, of a cover of *The New York Review of Books*) or an appeal he had made to calm student fears and tensions shortly after the May 4 shooting. Also indicted was Craig Morgan, the moderate prelaw student who, as president of the Kent State student government, spent the summer of 1970 trying to restore a sense of community and build bridges between campus and community.

To insulate the grand jury report from public criticism and debate, the Common Pleas judge issued two protective injunctions. The first forbade witnesses before the grand jury to make any public statement about the proceedings. The second prohibited demonstrations against the grand jury in the vicinity of the Portage County courthouse. The first order contained a single exception allowing President White one press conference, after which his lips were indefinitely sealed. In October 1970, two persons did speak out on opposite sides of the grand jury issue: Seabury Ford, a special county prosecutor appointed for the case, and Professor

Glen Frank, secretary of the faculty senate. Both were cited for contempt of court.

At that point, a group of witnesses and other Kent students brought the matter before the United States District Court in Cleveland. Early in November 1970, a federal judge held both injunctions unconstitutional and ordered them lifted. Apart from the highly unusual procedure of restricting public discussion of matters of great public importance, the judge found vital First Amendment rights of expression infringed upon by such broad restraints. The opinion was also critical of the grand jury's approach: "The report of the special grand jury . . . goes far beyond considerations of the offenses on which the indictments are based. . . . It condemns the conduct of the university officials and certain professors and students thereof and seriously draws into question the very delicate matter of academic freedom. . . . Publication of the report of the special grand jury has opened the social, political, and moral questions posed therein to debate in the public forum. . . . [T]he order prevents not only the three hundred [witnesses] from speaking but the rest of the world from hearing."

When the federal court removed the gag, the grand jury report became fair game for public comment. One of the first to exercise this newly recognized right of free speech was President White. At the annual meeting of the National Association of State Universities and Land-Grant Colleges, White issued an unusually strong and bitter reply to the grand jury's report, characterizing it as "a prime example of a brewing national disaster" which, if pursued to its logical end, "would eventually destroy not only Kent State but all major universities in America." (The full text is reprinted on pp. 129–133.) In the report's critique of the Kent administration, White found an ominous assault on the whole prevailing philosophy of American academic governance, "a frightening misunderstanding of the role and mission of higher education in our society."

The report was again challenged on January 25, 1971, by a special ad hoc committee. The committee submitted a detailed report to the Kent State University Faculty Senate. Although the committee touched on many facets of the report, its major criticisms were directed against the parts of the grand jury report which charged the faculty twenty-three with laxity. (These portions of the report are quoted at length on pp. 139–144.)

The most direct and forceful challenge to the grand jury report came in October and November 1970 in the federal courts. A group of persons indicted or cited by the grand jury brought suit in the United States District Court in Cleveland, seeking on constitutional grounds to have the report expunged and the prosecutions under it permanently enjoined. Several days of testimony were taken late in November 1970. Dozens of witnesses from the campus described under oath the fear and anxiety the grand jury report had instilled; several faculty members testified explicitly to modifications they had made in the teaching of their courses because of this threat.

On January 28, 1971, District Judge William K. Thomas handed down an opinion severely critical of the conduct of the grand jury and the special prosecutors. (Excerpts of his decision are quoted at length on pp. 134–138.) Although the decree stopped short of enjoining the prosecutions, it did order that all official copies of the report be expunged and destroyed. (The order left standing a few technical portions of the report, but decreed the deletion of all its narrative and analytical passages.)

The substance of the opinion was more important to the Kent academic community than the order itself. Much of the decision had to do with technical rules governing the conduct of grand jury investigations, noting that the Kent inquiry had violated numerous provisions of Ohio law. Toward the end of the opinion, however, Thomas came to the heart of the controversy between campus and local government. Having heard extensive testimony from faculty members and students, he concluded: "The report is dulling classroom discussion and is upsetting the teaching atmosphere. . . . [It] abridges the exercise of protected expression by the plaintiffs, who are members of the Kent State University faculty." Particularly disturbing to Thomas was "the candid and credited testimony of members of the faculty" who "because of the report

. . . have altered or dropped course materials for fear of classroom controversy." There were striking examples to support the generalization: an English professor, for example, who had eliminated poems by Yeats, Byron, and Arnold after reading the report.

Thomas accordingly held that the grand jury had impermissibly undermined academic freedom as well as violating Ohio law: "A university professor may add or subtract course content for different reasons. But when a university professor is fearful that one of the deleted poems may produce 'inflammatory discussion' in a poetry class, it is evident that the report's riptide is washing away protected expression on the Kent campus. . . . When thought is controlled or appears to be controlled, when pedagogues and pupils shrink from free inquiry at a state university because of a report of a resident grand jury, then academic freedom of expression is impermissibly impaired. This will curb conditions essential to fulfillment of the university's learning purposes."

The district court judgments were reviewed by the federal court of appeals in the fall of 1971 with the prosecutions held in abeyance awaiting the result. The appellate court sustained Judge Thomas with regard to the expungement of the grand jury report. Several weeks later, the clerk of the Portage County courts placed the official copy of the report in a wastebasket in the courthouse parking lot and touched a match to it. Thus ended the official life of an exceedingly controversial—and highly damaging—document.

The court also, however, upheld the refusal to quash the indictments, but reversed the district court's dissolution of the gag order, apparently feeling that the common pleas judge had acted properly in seeking to safeguard the impartiality of the criminal trial. Several months later, the Supreme Court reviewed the gag issue, concluding that the district court should now dismiss the case as moot—apparently because there was no longer any controversy about the right to criticize the grand jury.

Soon after the court of appeals had upheld the validity of the state court indictments, the prosecution began to call cases for trial. The selection of a jury for the first case was a long and difficult affair, presaging a lengthy and controversial criminal process.

In fact, however, the matter barely got beyond the threshold. The jury convicted the first defendant of a misdemeanor (in connection with the firebombing of the ROTC building). Charges against the second defendant were dropped because of a lack of evidence. Two other defendants pleaded guilty to a lesser offense. A fifth was acquitted by the jury. Then, unexpectedly, the attorney general of Ohio announced that charges against all remaining defendants were being dropped for lack of evidence. No explanation was given for this decision. The state had presumably led with what it believed to be its strongest cases and had fared poorly. Perhaps, too, public sentiment had moderated somewhat since the grand jury's report. Moreover, the arrival of a new Democratic administration in Columbus may have tempered the perspective on the whole Kent affair.

There the matter ended, with no prospect that these charges can be revived. The net effect of the grand jury's excesses is hard to assess. In some respects, external criticism may have helped to solidify Kent campus feeling. In 1969, few would have accused President White of being too soft on radicals or demonstrators. Indeed, the handling of the SDS, CCC, and Music and Speech Building incidents gave him the reputation of a hardliner. But the grand jury's extreme attack upon him for being "permissive" and "lax" in handling student discipline, outside speakers, and registration of student organizations, rapidly shifted the locus of concern. Support for the president appeared to develop from unexpected quarters.

Before leaving the subject of grand jury investigations, let us add something about the role of the federal government. A federal inquiry was held at Jackson but none at Kent; but that difference is perhaps the least significant datum. (Excerpts from the report are reprinted in Appendix H.) When the Mississippi federal grand jury was convened in the summer of 1970, the charge given by Judge Harold Cox (see pp. 166–168) left little doubt about his views of the matter: "No person participating in a riot or civil disorder or open combat with civil authorities, or failing to disperse on order of such authorities, or failing to immediately disassociate himself from such a group or gathering, has any civil right to expect to avoid serious injury or even death when the disorder becomes such as to require extreme measures and harsh treatment." Understandably, the grand jury met only briefly and recessed without handing down any indictments against police officers. (Judge Cox ordered a recess because he was about to leave on an extended trip to the Union of South Africa.) The justice department announced in November that the grand jury would resume consideration of the Jackson events at an undisclosed time in December 1970. There is no record, however, of any further action; surely, no indictments were ever issued, and because of the secrecy of grand jury proceedings (a secrecy violated by the Portage County report), we shall probably never know whether any action was even considered at the winter session.

More than a year after the killings, John Mitchell, attorney general of the United States, announced that he would not even convene a federal grand jury to consider the Kent deaths. Several reports which appeared during those months—an internal campus commission minority report, James Michener's study, analyses by I. F. Stone of the FBI report, a report done for the legal department of a national church group, and, most important, the Scranton Commission report—contained hints of an agreement among some guardsmen to turn and fire upon reaching the crest of the hill or to conceal the truth after the event or both. Yet Mitchell announced on August 13, 1971, that no federal grand jury would be impanelled to investigate the matter. He explained[1] that a review within the Justice Department persuaded him that "there is no credible evidence of a conspiracy between National Guardsmen to shoot students and that there is no likelihood of successful prosecutions of individual guardsmen." Although accepting the Scranton Commission's view that the student deaths had been "unnecessary, unwarranted, and inexcusable," Mitchell declared that further federal action would be inappropriate. In view of the "massive federal investigative resources already committed," he concluded, "further

[1] *New York Times*, Aug. 14, 1971.

investigation by a federal grand jury could not reasonably be expected to produce any new evidence which would contribute further to making a prosecutive judgment."

The Kent State University community has been unwilling to let the issue die. Shortly after the new president, Glenn Olds, assumed office in the fall of 1971, he took to Washington and delivered to the White House a petition signed by 10,380 Kent students, asking for a federal grand jury. Recognizing the probable finality of Mitchell's decision, Olds admitted to a reporter that the petition "has as much chance as a snowball in hell." Yet Olds and many others insisted that campus morale required clarification of the lingering doubts, some forum in which the interests of the university community might be vindicated. Interestingly, several attorneys defending persons indicted by the state grand jury strongly oppose a federal grand jury, which they fear might return fresh indictments against their clients rather than shifting the focus to the National Guard, state, and local officials. In any case, little likelihood exists that such an investigation will ever take place.

Both Kent and Jackson became keenly security conscious after the events of May 1970. A national wire-service reporter visiting Jackson State on registration day in the fall of 1970 was startled by the new, high fence running along both sides of Lynch Street. To the students, he observed, the fence had "the symbolism of a Berlin wall." Visitors to Kent came away with a similar impression of new and much tighter precautions. Three kinds of changes were evident on both campuses: (a) increases in security personnel; (b) restricted access to the campus; and (c) administrative changes.

Expenditures on campus security and police personnel have increased sharply. President White reported to the Ohio Senate Judiciary Committee in July 1971 that at Kent, the total cost of security rose from $519,963 in 1969–1970 to $1,018,588 the following year. There seems to have been less dramatic increases in both personnel and costs at Jackson. But security expenditures appear to have caused a reallocation of priorities, with academic interests the losers in both cases. At Kent, it is believed that a sharp curtailment in funds for travel to professional conventions in 1970–

1971 resulted from the increased security budget. At Jackson, the relationship is clearer: Four persons newly appointed to the faculty found their contracts suddenly cancelled in the late summer of 1970. The official explanation was that the contracts were never properly processed and that a reexamination of the personnel budget found these funds more urgently needed for new campus security positions. (One of the four, Dr. Kenneth Rainey, brought suit in the federal district court with the aid of the AAUP. The trial judge dismissed the case for lack of jurisdiction, apparently finding no possible denial of constitutional rights because the plaintiff was white. The court of appeals for the fifth circuit reversed the decision and sent the case back for trial, finding that Rainey had alleged a denial of his academic freedom and rights of free expression sufficient to warrant a judgment in his favor if he proved his case. The court cited many United States Supreme Court decisions involving academic freedom claims to which it deemed Rainey's suit analogous.)

Access to both campuses has also been restricted in this security-conscious mood. Jackson has built the fence which at last closes Lynch Street to traffic—but which some students feel makes the campus appear "like a cage." Kent's approach has been more complex. At the start of the 1970 summer session, President White issued tight security regulations. All visitors to the campus were asked to register at the drive or gate by which they entered and to carry identification passes while on campus. (Because of the ease of access to the campus, however, the enforcement of this rule depended almost entirely upon voluntary compliance.) The procedures were relaxed for the fall term, but visitors at night were still asked to register, and each student was required to carry an elaborate color-coded identification card at all times. Most campus events were closed to nonuniversity personnel. Demonstrations were required to be registered twenty-four hours in advance.

Both campuses were especially anxious during the memorial activities in May, 1971. While students listened to speeches by Charles Evers and other black leaders, Jackson State officials imposed a rigid bar against the press during the observance. Kent was less apprehensive than Jackson about outsiders during the commemorative period, although the ID card system remained in force. (Precautions were perhaps well taken. There was no violence during the four days of speeches and memorial services, but one thousand students did stage a twenty-four-hour peaceful sit-in at the new ROTC site.)

The internal reorganization which occurred during the summer and fall of 1970 also seems to reflect a security emphasis. At Kent, there has been faculty and student uneasiness about the creation of the new office of executive assistant to the president for emergency operations, the powers of which appear to be extensive but not precisely defined. Student and faculty consultation has been limited in the restructuring. Jackson's administrative response has been more modest. During the first week of classes after the school reopened, President Peoples announced the creation of a joint faculty-student "emergency council" to deal with potential trouble. Its powers, like those of Kent's new executive asisstant, still appear loosely defined, and its relation to the regular organs of student and faculty self-government in time of crisis are unclear.

The record of the ensuing year is not all ominous, however. Some hopeful internal reform has occurred on both campuses. At Kent, the changes are visible: a corps of protest marshals, made up of students, faculty, and townspeople; a special telephone system that alerts all campus buildings in case of trouble; and closer relations with state and local police agencies and detailed contingency plans. Additional steps were noted by a *Chronicle of Higher Education* reporter returning to the Kent campus a year after the tragedy: establishment of a speakers' area on the site of the burned out ROTC building; appointment of a student ombudsman, who served as a channel for student grievances; expansion of a small "house organ" into a newspaper distributed to faculty, staff, students, and townspeople; and a series of informal discussion meetings between faculty members and students in residence halls and faculty homes.

Finally, and perhaps most important, was the elevation to the presidency in September 1971 of Glenn A. Olds. Committed to restoring a sense of community and purpose, Olds has already taken important steps. During the winter of 1971–1972, he announced the creation of an institutional governance committee, including members of the board of trustees, faculty, students, administrative staff, and alumni. The task of the committee is to review various possible models and recommend a governance structure most appropriate to Kent State's needs in the 1970s. Meanwhile, important work is being done by the Center for Peaceful Change, including the creation of a new lecture series to bring significant speakers to the campus to commemorate the tragedy of May 4. There are, in short, many indications of continued effort by the members of the Kent campus community to overcome the lingering repercussions of 1970.

In both Ohio and Mississippi, moreover, conflicts have resulted between state and local and federal agencies. The most serious point of dispute, of course, was the controversy about sniper fire. Soon after the shootings, Guard officials in Ohio and policemen at Jackson both insisted that sniper shots had preceded their own volleys into the crowd. The Federal Bureau of Investigation immediately launched inquiries into that and other questions. By the middle of July, a preliminary FBI report enabled Assistant Attorney General for Civil Rights Jerris Leonard to report publicly that no substantial evidence of sniper fire had been discovered at either campus. That report drew sharp criticism from high officials in both states.

The controversy continues at several levels. Both the Hinds County and Portage County grand juries accepted the policemen's claims of sniper fire despite the federal reports. The Scranton Commission took a cautious view in both reports, finding no credible evidence of a sniper at Kent and the bare possibility of two shots fired from a window at Jackson. But at neither campus did the commission find the main volley justified by whatever provocation may have preceded it. Moreover, in neither case was the firing confined to the direction of the supposed sniper.

Another major conflict between federal and state or local authority occurred at Jackson. The bullet-riddled glass-and-metal panel on the front of Alexander Hall quickly became a vital piece of evidence. The holes in the panel would indicate the direction from which shots had been fired and would confirm or deny the sniper rumor. Students and other blacks were deeply upset at the threatened prospect of the removal of the panel by city or state police because that would almost certainly mean its destruction. Friction continued during the week after the shooting. Finally, a predawn compromise was effected on May 23, 1970, between President Peoples and Governor Williams, who was persuaded not to use National Guardsmen to disperse students or to remove the panel. Accordingly, representatives of the students supervised removal of the panel by state workmen on the assurance that all the fragments would be turned over—as the federal court of appeals had ordered —to the FBI for safekeeping and further study. Thus, a serious potential student-police and federal-state confrontation was narrowly avoided at the last moment.

At least one ameliorative change has been made in direct response to the events of May. On May 30, barely two weeks after the Jackson incident, the executive director of the Mississippi Law-Enforcement Assistance Division announced a new regulation designed to restrict the use of firearms by police departments. Any law-enforcement agency seeking a grant for the purchase of lethal weapons must now show it has "command-and-control procedures," assuring proper restraint in riot conditions. (The retroactive effect, if any, of this new stricture on weapons already acquired is unclear.) Special emphasis is also being given to training in the use of lethal weapons, the proper deployment of such weapons, and a command-and-control procedure when dealing with civil disturbances and riots. Apparently, however, little has been done to ensure the use of *nonlethal* weapons under such circumstances. (The grand jury report and other pressures, as we noted earlier, brought about the dismissal of the Jackson police chief who was in charge at the time of the campus killings. In his place came a twenty-year veteran of the force, Lavell Tullos, who instituted a code of conduct for Jackson police officers which demands respectful treatment of all persons regardless of "race, color, status in life, or ethnic background."

73

Robert M. O'Neil

Tullos also issued a one-hundred-page civil-disturbance operation plan, which reflects [in the mayor's words] "the most modern, up-to-date methods of crowd control," and which contains explicit precautions against a repetition of the volley against Alexander Hall.) (Clearly not satisfied with the modest reforms in the year after the killings, five Democratic Senators on May 18, 1971, asked the secretary of defense for a report on steps taken by the National Guard to prevent a recurrence of the Kent tragedy. There has been no formal news of a response.)

Certain consequences of the May events are unique to Ohio and must therefore be treated separately, for example, the role of the Federal Bureau of Investigation. Within hours after the shooting, the Portage County chapter of the American Civil Liberties Union telegraphed Attorney General Mitchell urging that the FBI be sent to Kent to investigate. Federal agents were dispatched almost at once. Two weeks later, the ACLU chapter was again in touch with the Justice Department, this time trying as hard to have the agents withdrawn as they had earlier sought to have them called in. This sharp reversal occurred because the FBI inquiry focused increasingly on the conduct and teaching practices of several members of the faculty. Numerous students and the professors were asked searching questions about the conduct of classes, about political and social opinions, and even about purely private, off-campus conduct. Senator Stephen Young of Ohio charged that the FBI was not only asking improper questions of persons on the campus but was enrolling agents as "plants" in summer and fall courses. (Although FBI Director J. Edgar Hoover had admitted the interrogations, the charges of planting agents in classrooms has neither been acknowledged nor been conclusively proved.)

It is difficult to assess the blame for this improper police surveillance. FBI agents needed and obtained the cooperation of some university official to examine class lists of the courses taught by the several suspected professors. (Had these lists not been voluntarily tendered, they might later have been obtained by compulsory process anyway as happened with membership lists of student organizations on several campuses.)

Moreover, the same FBI agents who conducted the Kent investigation also undermined the theory that guardsmen responded to sniper fire. To the agents there was presumably little difference between the two lines of interrogation, the one of eyewitnesses to the shooting on the hillside, the other of eyewitnesses to alleged classroom incitement, political rallies, and campus meetings. The distinction is critical, if subtle, and is central to an understanding of academic freedom. For government to ask questions about a public event, such as an armed confrontation between students and police, intrudes upon no collegial relationship and breaches no professional confidence. The fact that the object of the inquiry occurred on a college campus is for this purpose irrelevant. But, for a police officer to obtain class lists from a university official and then to proceed systematically to ask students what their professors said in class about controverial topics strikes at a central nerve of academic freedom and integrity. Although the process of inquiry is functionally similar in both cases, the effects are vastly different.

One measure of the complexity of Kent's aftermath is the volume and diversity of litigation filed during the ensuing year. A pamphlet issued by the American Civil Liberties Union listed eight legal actions pending or about to be filed as of early 1971. These complaints seek to recover civil damages from state officials for the wrongful death of one of the students killed on May 4; to enjoin future use of the National Guard on Ohio campuses under similar conditions and to assure that when summoned they will carry non-lethal weapons; to enjoin further surveillance by FBI and other law-enforcement agencies on the Kent campus; to declare unlawful the dormitory search and to recover the student's possessions that were seized; to quash the criminal indictments brought by the Portage County Grand Jury; and to have students declared eligible to vote in Kent without having to swear a life-long intent to remain in the county.

The disposition of several of these actions has been noted above. Two other developments in the courts are worthy of note. In the first of the wrongful-death civil suits to be appealed, the trial court was found to have erred in dismissing the claim filed by the father of one of the slain Kent students. The lower court had relied upon the ancient doctrine of sovereign immunity in finding the state government beyond the reach of such suits; the appellate court, however, reversed the decision, but the Ohio Supreme Court held that the dismissal of the suit was proper.

The federal courts rendered one other decision of importance. Shortly after the shooting, a group of Kent State students brought suit challenging the constitutionality of state laws permitting the deployment of National Guard units in campus civil disorders. The suit specifically attacked the use and the actions of guard contingents at Kent in May 1970. The court of appeals concluded that the basic laws were valid but reversed a district court decision which had dismissed the complaint outright. The higher court sent the matter back to the trial court for further proceedings and the taking of evidence on two questions—first, whether the training given to the Ohio National Guard either required or made inevitable the use of fatal force during a campus disorder; and second, whether the particular actions of the guardsmen on May 4, 1970, were a violation of individual constitutional rights. The appellate court insisted on both issues that "the right to be heard is itself a constitutional right of vital importance."

The search of Kent dormitory rooms in the days after the shooting had also been challenged in the federal courts with the help of the American Civil Liberties Union. Dormitory residents argued that because their contracts extended through June, any unauthorized search before the end of the school year violated the constitutional right of privacy. Prosecutor Kane, who had supervised the search, claimed that the campus had been vacated when the entry occurred. In June 1972, a federal district judge in Cleveland —the same judge who ordered the grand jury report destroyed— held in favor of the plaintiffs, finding that the officers' action "violated the Fourth Amendment rights of the students whose rooms were searched."

Litigation was less extensive in Mississippi than in Ohio. Mention has already been made of the Rainey case, perhaps the most important to be filed in the aftermath of the tragedy. Meanwhile, relatives of the two dead youths and three wounded students filed suits in the federal district court for southern Mississippi seeking $13.8 million in damages. The mayor and other city officials were originally joined but were dismissed from the case, leaving as defendants only a group of law-enforcement officers. Late in March 1972, the all-white jury found in favor of the defendants on all counts after two full days of deliberation. The verdict came as no surprise to Mississippi blacks, who had paid little attention to the case and (as Fayette Mayor Charles Evers summarized the reaction) assumed that no redress could come from an all-white jury. Presumably, no other avenue of recourse now exists.

Not all government response has taken place in the courts. In Ohio, at least, there have been important administrative and legislative repercussions. Early in the summer of 1970, the Ohio Board of Regents amended its regulations governing the allocation of appropriated funds to the state colleges and universities. The revised rule provided that if any campus closed voluntarily or was closed as a result of disorder, the flow of public funds to that campus would be reduced proportionately. This new policy posed an obvious dilemma for administrators: On the one hand, the threat of losing state subvention might tend to resolve doubts in favor of remaining open in troubled times, even though closing was the wiser course. On the other hand, this new regulation gave to external agencies—courts and prosecuting attorneys like those who obtained and issued the Kent injunction on May 4—the power not only to shut a state-supported institution but to bankrupt it as well. It is unlikely that administrative officials will commit fiscal suicide by closing unless absolutely necessary; it is less clear whether local officials who have effective power to bar and lock college gates may not use for personal or political gain the vastly increased leverage this revision affords them.

The Ohio legislature also responded to the wave of campus unrest by adopting a disruption law and by creating a special interim legislative committee. As originally passed by the lower chamber, House Bill 1219 provided for the automatic suspension of a faculty member upon his arrest for a broad range of state crimes, on or off the campus, and for his automatic dismissal upon conviction. To secure the concurrence of the senate, the bill was modified to provide that the arrest of a faculty member (or student or staff member) initiates a hearing before a referee (an attorney designated by the regents, who must practice in the county but may not be associated with the university). An adverse judgment by the referee on the charges warrants suspension without pay pending the resolution of the criminal case, though a discretionary probation is possible.

If the defendant is convicted, dismissal from the universtiy follows automatically without any further proceedings. If he is acquitted, then reinstatement follows, but without retroactive amends to cover the suspension period. Conviction, moreover, carries serious collateral consequences. A faculty or staff member dismissed from a state-supported or state-aided institution may not be hired by any other such institution for a period of one year. Even after that time, reemployment elsewhere in the state system is contingent upon express approval of the governing board.

Ohio House Bill 1219 contains a number of other important provisions. It creates a new and loosely defined crime of "disruption"—designed to impose special disabilities on those who commit certain acts on college and university campuses. Under the law, one may be arrested for joining an assemblage contrary to a curfew order of the university president or governing board. The administrative judgment that there is a sufficient emergency to trigger the vast range of discretion appears unreviewable, either in the suspension hearing that follows an arrest or in the eventual criminal prosecution.

On June 1, 1970, in order to determine what further legislation, if any, was warranted, the 108th Ohio General Assembly created a Select Committee to Investigate Campus Disturbances. Consisting of fifteen members from both houses, the committee broke into subcommittees for the purpose of holding hearings on public campuses throughout the state. The information-gathering process occupied much of the summer. In early October, the committee submitted its interim report (quoted at length on pp. 145–151)'. Although its conclusions and recommendations did not warrant optimism among the Ohio academic community, the report showed far greater understanding of the nature and functions of higher education than had the Portage County grand jury report.

In the area of student discipline, the committee found considerable laxity in enforcement of campus rules and wide variations among them. The report proposed codification and standardization of offenses and procedures among institutions and clearer authorization to use interim or summary suspension. (The report also reminded administrators that House Bill 1219 was intended to supplement, and not to replace, applicable state laws or campus rules.)

The committee also came down rather hard on the faculty. Among the pertinent findings: "Instances were reported where faculty members had condoned or actively encouraged disruptive activities by students and had even participated in such activities, had failed to teach the scheduled course content, had failed without excuse to meet scheduled classes, had made unwarranted or repeated use of obscene language in open class, and before other students had ridiculed and degraded students holding political and social opinions opposed to their own." Against this background, the committee was troubled to find "little or no enforcement or professional discipline," partly because the process of hiring and promotion had been unduly delegated to lower officials with insufficient supervision. The legislators deplored the practice of hiring senior faculty members initially to tenured positions without a probationary period. Yet, the committee report also gave attention to academic practices in need of improvement: the uneven quality of instruction, the tendency to stress research at the expense of teaching, especially of undergraduates; the inaccessibility to students of many senior professors; and the use of university facilities for research projects "which are either unrelated to the educational function or hinder its performance in some degree."

Other portions of the report dealt with university operations, campus security and law enforcement, and organized efforts to disrupt. Many of the recommendations were more a call for further study than for immediate action. The committee urged establishment of better campus communications, relief of overcrowding in residence halls and popular courses, better training and higher compensation and qualifications for campus security officers, clarification of lines of authority and responsibility, closer liaison between campus police and city or town government and more effective drug-abuse control programs. Only a few of the recommendations under these headings were controversial—for example, the suggestion that more efficient intelligence-gathering systems were needed or that tighter restrictions should be placed upon the access of non-members of the university community.

V

LESSONS, CONCLUSIONS, RECOMMEN- DATIONS

There are no heroes and few villains in this unhappy chronicle. There are people who made mistakes, some grave. There are other people who lost their lives as a result of those mistakes. Yet no matter how exceptional the misfortunes of May 1970, certain lessons of general value emerge. Accordingly, we feel it appropriate, indeed incumbent, to offer conclusions and recommendations.

We are mindful that other study groups, notably the President's Commission on Campus Unrest, have been far better equipped to find facts. The report of that commission most helpfully and eloquently casts light upon many dark corners of American higher education. We feel it unnecessary to duplicate the findings of that commission or to indicate concurrence with particular recommendations. Instead, we direct our proposals mainly at the faculty, students, and administrators of American colleges and universities, because our study has been chiefly concerned with the needs and interests of those constituencies. But, before offering our recommendations, we begin with a series of general conclusions and impressions about the state of American higher education in the early 1970s.

Academic autonomy is a fragile and vulnerable concept. The ability of a college or university to determine its own destiny necessarily depends heavily upon the grace and goodwill of external groups. Few, if any, viable legal safeguards protect or insulate the campus from even the most dangerous forms of external pressure. The defense of academic autonomy is seldom politically popular. Public officials who seek their own ends rather than those of the academy often prefer repression to protection. Private donors and benefactors are easily disappointed by the performance of institutions of higher learning to which they have contributed. Once lost, the vital confidence of taxpayers, legislators, parents, and donors is extremely hard to regain. Meanwhile, the campus remains perilously exposed to hostile forces in society that can advance selfish interests, allay irrational fears, or vindicate real or imagined grievances, by attacking academic freedom or autonomy. The university, largely because of its inability to retaliate, makes a convenient scapegoat for a broad range of anxieties. When many critical problems demand explanation, but defy solution, the pressures upon the academic community threaten to become intolerable.

Internal control of campus destiny has been progressively displaced by external forces. In the recent experience at both Kent State and Jackson State, we have seen graphic examples of the process of displacement. But the substitution of external control for internal governance has proceeded apace at many other institutions as well. The avenues of encroachment are many and varied: insidious and clandestine surveillance by law-enforcement agencies; grand jury proceedings which allow no opportunity for response or defense; court decisions compelling a campus to open or to close, to make up courses, or to refund tuition regardless of the internal resolutions; repressive legislation mandating certain actions contrary to internal consensus; and often uninformed executive and administrative decrees replacing the experienced judgment of professionals.

Although it is impossible for a campus to prevent intrusions by civil authorities, it is both feasible and essential to guard against such intervention. The unhappy experiences of Kent and Jackson demonstrate how relatively helpless the campus is against public officials who wish to violate its autonomy and who often have the legal authority to do so. If the governor wants to send the Guard or the mayor wants to assign the city police to campus duty, there is little the president can do to bar their entry. While external police are on the campus, they report to external officials and are not likely to take orders from university administrators. Yet, there are many precautions the president or chancellor can take to safeguard as much campus autonomy as remains under such conditions. Careful contingency planning should anticipate the armed camp situation that existed for several days at Kent or the sudden invasion that Jackson experienced on several occasions. The authority, the command, and the objectives of such external forces should be ascertained at once. That information should be widely disseminated to the entire campus community. All proper precautions should be taken to avoid confrontations between members of the campus community and the outside forces. Close liaison should be maintained between the civil authorities and the campus police or security office. In short, the president should retain control and direction of his own campus as long as possible, no matter how far his autonomy and authority appear to have been preempted.

Some of the gravest wounds to academic autonomy have been self-inflicted; the academic community bears at least partial blame for its plight. Campus officials, faculty, administrators, and students have been incredibly unsophisticated about the effects upon campus autonomy of seeking external assistance in times of trouble. The calling in of civil police to quell a disturbance carries risks. Frequently there has been overreaction on both sides, followed by escalation and polarization. The report of the National Commission on the Causes and Prevention of Violence noted in the summer of 1969: "Even in cases where the need for calling the civil police has been generally recognized, the degree of force actually employed has frequently been perceived as excessive by the majority of the campus community, whose sympathies then turned against the university authorities." Also, the police usually assume command of the field when they arrive. The decision whether to make arrests and in what manner is typically beyond the control of the dean and in the hands of a precinct captain, who may know little about colleges and students. After arrests have been made, the decision whether to prosecute and for what offense also passes beyond the university's control. More than one college official seeking clemency for his students had been reminded by a stern court that the interests of the state have superseded those of the academy.

The other self-inflicted wound is the use of the injunction. Superficially appealing as an alternative to calling the police, a court order against campus disruption has many drawbacks, the main one being the displacement of university discretion by judicial judgment. Moreover, the practical difficulty of affording adequate notice to persons potentially bound by the injunction has resulted in the invalidation of numerous contempt citations. The terms of an injunction drafted for one day's disorder may not fit tomorrow's needs—or if they do, the flexibility that facilitates such adaptation may render the order unconstitutionally vague. Thus, the ready resort of campuses to court injunctions has sometimes proved unwise and even (as at the State University of New York at Buffalo) unlawful. In every instance, however, the delegation to a judge or jury of critical and sensitive decisions about campus governance sets a dangerous precedent. Such abdication may also impair institutional autonomy in other contexts.

Grave threats to academic autonomy also arise from the unofficial activities of vigilante groups, extremists of both right and left.

Official and self-inflicted wounds to campus autonomy are at least relatively easily understood. Far more complex are the shadowy, often anonymous attacks mounted by extremist groups within and around the academic community. The months since May 1970 produced alarming increases in such vigilante activity against which the campus is virtually helpless. Twice, annual meetings of the Association for the Advancement of Science have been disrupted and speakers prevented from speaking by a radical caucus.

In the summer and fall of 1970, Lawrence, Kansas, a major Midwestern state-university town, lived in growing fear of forays by vigilante groups on the right. Speakers at a dozen or more campuses have been hooted, jeered at, and even physically hustled off the stage because members of the campus community found their views and policies abhorrent. At the same time, right-wing groups have infiltrated or spied upon controversial campus political activities and have condoned physical attacks upon young persons whose hair length, style of dress, or speech they could not tolerate.

The campus is caught helplessly between these vicious adversaries. The university is properly a battleground for opposing ideas and ideologies. But it cannot long survive as the target of enemies who back their ideologies with fists and firebombs. An authoritarian institution can withstand such conflicts for a time, but no free institution thus beset can long flourish. The qualities of a university that are its strength—tolerance for dissent and invitation to controversy—make it vulnerable when basic respect for academic values and procedures is absent. Under such conditions, the campus can survive only by assuming a paramilitary organization, by suspending the civil liberties and academic freedom of its members, by according distorted priority to security concerns, and the like. In short, the *forms* of a university can be preserved in such circumstances only at grave cost to the *substance*.

The shootings at Kent and Jackson cannot be blamed upon faulty campus governance; nonetheless, different structures and more effective internal communication than existed before May 1970 might have substantially reduced the risks. For reasons we have reviewed at some length, another internal-governance struc-

85

ture might not have spared either institution from confrontation with hostile, armed officers. Yet, critical weaknesses existed in governance and communication on both campuses just before the events of May 1970. Improvements and alternatives have emerged from this analysis and the work of other study groups; indeed, in the case of Kent, major reforms had already been proposed in the fall of 1969 by the AAUP's special committee of inquiry, but apparently were not implemented. Kent and Jackson are neither better nor worse in regard to governance than most other comparable institutions of higher learning. The lessons of May 1970 should therefore not be lost in other colleges which would have been similarly unable to avert disaster under like circumstances.

The internal communication systems of universities are poorly suited to emergency conditions. More effective means for disseminating urgent messages exist in other institutions that have recently had less need for them—summer camps, high schools, prisons, military bases, and the like. Of course, we are not suggesting that the college campus emulate these rigid institutions in communications any more than in governance. Nonetheless, valuable lessons and techniques might be borrowed from analogous experience in other contexts. Media are needed which are responsible both to crisis conditions and the needs of academic freedom.

Campus disorder is characteristically followed not by major institutional reform but by superficial and sometimes counterproductive changes. The increased security consciousness at both Kent and Jackson during the summer of 1970 reflects a now familiar pattern of response to campus violence. Even where major weaknesses in governance and communication have either brought about violence or been revealed by it, the immediate pressures for institutional first aid are usually so compelling that energy and funds are initially used for short-run repairs. Top priority is given to expanding the police force, issuing and checking student ID cards, excluding unwanted outsiders, and similar security measures. By the time the initial shock has abated, other concerns have again preempted scarce time and resources. Little is done to remedy underlying defects in governance or communication. Meanwhile, the measures taken in response to campus violence may be counterproductive. If one seeks to restore harmony and confidence to a divided and troubled campus, the doubling of the number of blue uniforms and black cars seen by students may increase rather than reduce tensions.

Despite the lessons of Kent and Jackson, it is unrealistic to expect the disarmament of police assigned to campus duty. There is much basis for hope that the events of May 1970 will recur neither in Ohio nor in Mississippi. Greater emphasis has been placed by responsible officials in both states on the use of nonlethal weapons. Provision has been made by the federal government for improved riot-control training of National Guardsmen and for equipment more appropriate to crowd control than to foreign invasion. But the gains are slight and the assurances tenuous. Two recent developments suggest *how* tenuous. During the summer of 1970, legislation was proposed in the United States Senate to require presidential approval to load the weapons of National Guardsmen on domestic riot duty. The proposal was defeated by a vote of 87 to 2, only Senators Kennedy and McCarthy supporting it. Meanwhile, no basic policy change has been made at the national level; the critical judgment about armament thus may remain with the battlefield commander, depending on state policy.

The second event seems more ominous. A month to the day after the Kent tragedy, the mayor of Honolulu announced that city policemen sent to any troubled campus on the island of Oahu would go unarmed on the principle "that law and order should be tempered with justice and not with force." The response was hostile, not only from the police department but also from the Hawaii Government Employees Association, which quickly filed a suit challenging the mayor's judgment. Even the president of the University of Hawaii was skeptical, finding this an "artificial" and "political" controversy. The mayor's proposal received no support from any quarter.

Although the Indochina war has been a major catalyst to student unrest, the termination of the war is unlikely to assure campus tranquility. In general, we share the Scranton Commission's view[1] that in order to restore harmony "nothing is more important than an end to the war in Indochina. Disaffected students see the war as a symbol of moral crisis in the nation which, in their eyes, deprives even the law of its legitimacy."

It is essential now to look to the future against the background of this unhappy recent past. If there is to be disorder in the future, whatever the cause, will we be better prepared to deal effectively and responsibly with it than we were in the spring of 1970? It is in the context of this inquiry that we offer our recommendations and suggestions.

Our conclusions and recommendations follow under two distinct headings concerning: the faculty and the administration. We begin with the faculty because we believe that the faculty has a vital role to play—perhaps the most vital role—in events of the kind we have reviewed here.

A university is among the most vulnerable institutions in our society. Because of its vulnerability, it is a tempting target for those who want to destroy the institutions of our society. One may wish to destroy the Dow Chemical Company, but find himself unable to do so. One may wish to disrupt the workings of the Department of Defense, but find himself unable to do so. Disrupting classes, defacing libraries, and closing university buildings is easier. The university is vulnerable for the same reasons that lead us to cherish it. It is dedicated to the open expression of dissenting opinion and to the free examination of competing ideas.

The immediate threat to the university community is probably considerably more subtle than burning buildings. The university can be weakened more seriously from loss or impairment of its functions than from loss of its buildings. If enough people become convinced that the teaching of accumulated knowledge is irrelevant and that scholarly research consists of fiddling while Rome burns, then we may wind up with university buildings, but they will be hollow of intellectual activity.

[1] *Special Report of the President's Commission on Campus Unrest: The Killings at Jackson State,* 1970.

No Heroes, No Villains

When too much of the everyday life of our society is characterized by incivility, surely we do not want to prescribe as a cure the suspension of our work in art, literature, and music. When we want to protest the encroaching forces of pollution in our environment, surely we can come up with a more creative gesture than closing the engineering school. When we are faced with racial tensions and misunderstandings, metropolitan taxation, and a lack of responsiveness by public officials to their constituents, we in the university cannot responsibly suggest that our noblest contribution toward meeting these challenges lies in the cancelling of classes in sociology, economics, and political science.

Our central proposition is clear and simple. The faculty of every college and university must make a deep commitment not only to keep its institution open, but to maintain the institution's freedom and preserve its autonomy. Several subsidiary propositions follow from this central premise.

(1) The faculty has a legitimate and substantial stake in the governance of their college or university. That stake is not lost or diminished when the institution is in trouble from within or without. On the contrary, faculty participation becomes essential when decisions of vast implication and great hazard must be made quickly. It is vital to reaffirm the nature and extent of this commitment; there is some evidence of ambivalence on the part of many professors toward participation in university government.

(2) The faculty has a specific responsibility—to themselves and to other constituencies of the university—to assure significant participation in decisions regarding law enforcement and security. This role subsumes a broad range of decisions. Obviously, it includes the calling in of external police forces, both the making of the actual decision to seek such aid and the method by which that decision is to be made. This responsibility may also extend to the organization, training, reporting, and even the equipment (including weapons) of a campus police force.

(3) The faculty has a responsibility to encourage and to ensure the participation of other constituencies in the development of security measures and systems. If the faculty does not care and

does not press the issue, it is unlikely that students or nonacademic staff will play any role in such matters, even though they share with faculty and administration a vital concern for the institution's welfare and autonomy.

(4) The faculty has an obligation to ensure effective internal communication on the campus in times of tension and crisis. At one level, professors are among the most effective communicators of vital information, especially to students. In times of stress, forums are available in which a faculty voice may dispel a rumor, supply correct information, or disseminate truth with the esteem and credibility that faculty alone command.

(5) The faculty has a responsibility to deter violence and destruction within a university community. Better than any other members of the university community, professors should appreciate how damaging violence is to academic institutions and values and how alien it is to the search for truth and understanding paramount in a university This precept does not mean that professors should put their bodies on the line or engage in physical combat with students. Many simply could not assume such a role, and many others would not feel it appropriate to do so even if they could. Instead, there are many ways in which faculty members may help to preserve or restore order—by serving as marshals and observers in times of turbulence; by speaking out against violence; by counselling and cautioning students with whom they have special rapport; and by providing alternatives to violence in the solution of university problems.

(6) Faculty has a responsibility to help rebuild the sense of community within a university after divisive forces have polarized it. Following every disorder, there remains a major job of reconstruction before the university can regain its former strength. It is essential for faculty to assume a dominant role in the task of rebuilding, for they have the experience necessary for that task and a major stake in its success.

(7) Faculty has a responsibility to explain academic institutions and the academic profession to the nonacademic world. There is much misunderstanding of the university and the professoriat in

the United States; many citizens believe the worst about the academic profession because they do not know the facts. Hostility born of such misunderstanding will persist until the professoriat finds ways of communicating with the surrounding community more effectively than it has done in the past. Methods might include speakers' bureaus (with reasonable assurance of reaching receptive audiences); letters and articles in nonacademic publications; and organized public-information campaigns designed to explain the academy to the outside world.

(8) Faculty should become increasingly vigilant in the protection of its own academic interests. As the incidence of legislation and administrative action directed against faculty mounts, the need for defensive or protective measures grows. Faculty organizations should seek, as the AAUP has done for some years, to keep abreast of developments in state legislatures that affect academic freedom. Faculty organizations should work more closely with other groups which might join forces in sponsoring or opposing legislation, in bringing test cases to challenge repressive laws or decrees, in filing briefs in pending cases, and in gathering the information needed for intelligent self-protection. Civil rights and civil liberties organizations, labor groups, student associations, and organizations of librarians and other affected professionals are potential but largely untapped allies.

(9) The faculty must continue to assume a major role in the articulation and enforcement of high professional standards. The academic profession has always been highly visible and (properly) held to unusually high standards in its role of education and leadership of youth. Albeit largely unpublicized, university teachers have assumed responsibility for self-regulation. Recently, these efforts have been redoubled with the promulgation by national and campus faculty groups of codes of professional responsibility. (The AAUP has long had a Committee B concerned with such standards.) One such code, adopted late in 1970 by the council of the national AAUP, underscores the need both for the articulation of ethical and conduct standards and for detecting and sanctioning breaches of those standards. Yet, there is a risk that these codes

will seem hollow and pious pronouncements to the critics of the professoriat without a persistent commitment to implementation. Appropriate steps designed to give vitality to such codes might include special seminars for the preparation and inauguration into the professoriat of beginning teachers; establishment of autonomous machinery by which to review charges of unprofessional or unethical faculty conduct; and the wide dissemination of periodic compliance reports.

This study also invites recommendations in the realm of administrative responsibility. We begin with a sense of urgency about the deteriorating relations between campus and community in many college towns and cities. Although we feel the faculty, students, and staff can do much to improve communication and understanding, ultimate responsibility for community-campus relations rests with the administration.

One general proposition seems central: The college or university must accept the full implications of citizenship—a unique citizenship—in the community of which it is a part. Institutions of higher learning have both the rights and the responsibilities of such citizenship. Often, the campus is the community's major purchaser of goods, employer of labor, provider of culture and entertainment, and yet its gravest potential threat to order and tranquility. A college or university is, in short, a mixed blessing for its neighbors. As the campus population grows and its borders impinge more directly upon the community, the potential for conflict increases. Under these conditions, the duties and perquisites of corporate citizenship demand a reevaluation of campus-community relationships. In this regard, we offer the following recommendations.

(1) The security needs of the campus and of the community should be examined together, recognizing the interdependence of the two entities, the essentiality of cooperation in matters of law enforcement, and the potential economies of collaboration. As we have observed at Kent and Jackson, rapid expansion of campus security forces has become almost a reflex response to student unrest. We share the concern which Fred M. Hechinger of the *New York Times* expressed in the fall of 1970: "Perhaps nothing so visibly symbolizes the changing nature of the campus and the threat to it

as an enclave of reason as the trend toward large university police forces. Apart from the deplorable waste of funds, this development . . . introduces the rule of force where controversies ought to be settled in honest debate and where, in fact, even unresolved controversies ought to be able to live side by side."

Moreover, the experience of universities such as Michigan suggests there is no inexorable logic in the creation of a separate campus police force. Ann Arbor appears to be the only Big Ten campus that has no large security force of its own, relying entirely upon the city for law enforcement. It is also one of the most peaceful and orderly of the major Midwestern universities. Whereas Wisconsin, Illinois, and other Big Ten institutions have steadily augmented their campus police forces, Michigan has avoided this heavy drain on its resources and retained close and important ties with the city government.

We urge that colleges and universities initiate a comprehensive reexamination of the security needs of the total community of which the campus is a part. Various options should be considered, ranging from completely separate police forces to a single, integrated agency. (State law may either require separate campus security forces or preclude town or city officers from patrolling state property. Where such obstacles exist, new legislation may be necessary but should not be impossible to obtain.) A careful review should be made of all security needs, independent as well as shared. Outside expert consultation may be summoned by communities wishing to reassess their security needs and redesign their forces. The resulting arrangement should equitably allocate costs between city and campus, should firmly fix responsibility and authority under a broad range of conditions (including emergencies), and should be publicized generally in both academic and nonacademic communities.

(2) Liaison officers should be appointed by both campus and community to work closely together in security planning and other areas of mutual concern. These officers should report directly to the highest level, the mayor or city manager on one side and the president or chancellor on the other. Selection should be made from among persons with close town-campus ties—citizens who are alumni or supporters of the college and faculty or staff members

who have substantial roots in the community. The two liaison officers should meet frequently, involving their colleagues and other officials as appropriate. The results of their joint deliberations should be publicized in an effort to increase on both sides the awareness of interdependence and of the extent of cooperation. There should be few secrets between these two persons but much candor in sharing criticisms by the constituents of each about the domain of the other. Members of the campus community should be encouraged (though not compelled) to take their grievances about the mayor and the town to the liaison officer rather than to the columns of the local newspaper, and vice versa. Occasional open meetings should be sponsored by the two officers to discuss and resolve grievances that merit public attention. Reports should be rendered periodically on action taken on citizen and campus complaints. Efforts should be made on both sides to strengthen the role of the liaison officer and to support his constructive work.

(3) The university should acknowledge the role of the community as a constituency of the total campus by affording community spokesmen a share in its governance. Almost everyone recognizes in principle that the community has an interest in the life of the university—a stake which it sometimes asserts unreasonably. Yet few institutions have made constructive attempts to involve community spokesmen in decisions that significantly affect external relations. The reasons for exclusion are many and varied, but the result has often been an increase in community suspicion, distrust, and misunderstanding—and thus, ultimately, far more damaging intrusions than would have come about through formalized invitations.

A few of the new universitywide senates contain seats for community representatives along with spokesmen for administration, students, faculty, staff, and alumni. But there are other possible forms of participation, such as the citizens-community advisory council that the University of California at Riverside and other campuses have successfully used both as a sounding board and as a channel of involvement in governance. Much imaginative thought is needed to develop ways of bringing community spokesmen into university governance and decision-making—regularly rather than sporadically in time of crisis, intelligently rather than blindly, and essentially on the university's terms. Opening the doors partially in this vital way may do much in the long run to bolster the autonomy of the campus.

(4) The university administration must avoid unwarranted delegation of authority to external bodies. We have spoken of the wounds inflicted by the needless calling of external police or by the resort to court injunctions. Of course, there are times when the police must be called, when it would be irresponsible for a campus administration to risk life and limb by riding out a rising storm. And there may be times when an injunction against unlawful acts on campus is warranted, despite its many hazards and the limited prospect of effective deterrence. At other times, however, administrators might decline to surrender essential control over the campus to external agencies if they are fully aware of the consequences. Accordingly, we suggest that every chief campus officer trace carefully the probable consequences of such a delegation and assess alternatives by which campus autonomy can be retained.

(5) Law-enforcement surveillance of faculty and student activities and the probing of confidential realtionships should be vigorously resisted. In the summer of 1970, the House Internal Security Committee sent questionnaires to 179 colleges and universities asking information about outside speakers during the preceding two years. The committee's apparent purpose was to establish that colleges, and especially student fees, are subsidizing radical activities by paying radical speakers. Soon after the request went out, the American Civil Liberties Union contacted all the respondent institutions, urging the presidents not to comply with a demand that threatened constitutional rights of members of the campus community. Some institutions told the committee they did not keep records of the information. Others did not reply at all. Only a handful—eight or ten—formally refused the committee's request. The great bulk of this sensitive information was garnered from unsuspecting or deferential campus administrators without the issuance of a single subpoena, despite the ACLU alert.

There are other examples of voluntary compliance with intrusive and dangerous surveillance. We have noted that the Kent State University administration simply gave the FBI the class lists

95

they sought so that agents could begin interrogating students about the teaching and, in some cases, the political views of their professors. We do not suggest that the response was exceptional; indeed, most registrars would probably have cooperated with a law-enforcement request almost as a matter of reflex. The great danger is not only that police will continue to seek this sort of information. The more alarming prospect is that college and university officials may often comply wtihout assessing the implications, legal alternatives, or possible safeguards and protections. Accordingly, although recognizing the need for appropriate cooperation with proper law-enforcement activity, we urge caution in the face of infiltration and interrogation that threaten the confidential relationship so essential to an academic community.

(6) No person should assume a position as president or chancellor without an understanding on security and police matters with the local government. We recognize, of course, the limited value of formal agreements that police will never be sent to the campus unsolicited. When parties or personnel change, or even when good will gives way to suspicion and distrust, such ententes may be repudiated at will. Clearly, they are not legally enforceable even though, in some abstract sense, they may have legal force.

(7) Members of the surrounding community should be invited to share a broad range of campus activities. If a university supports a major athletic program, the steady attendance of local citizens at games is not only desired but economically essential. Sometimes the community is invited to attend cultural and entertainment events on the campus, though priority in the allocation of scarce seats is usually given to internal applicants. When it comes to the primary function of the university—its educational programs— scant attention is given to the community. Where the population of the campus has become increasingly cosmopolitan (for example, if the old teachers' college with a once local faculty and student body has become a comprehensive state university with an international reputation) the apparent academic neglect of the town may seriously injure the feelings and wound the pride of local citizens and thus invite their anger.

No Heroes, No Villains

We suggest that this trend toward alienation and divorcement should be reversed by conscious programs and efforts. Such efforts might include special consideration to local high school graduates in the admission process and the earmarking of special financial aids for needy local youth; appointments to adjunct and even permanent faculty positions of practitioners in the community, who may have skill and experience to offer students as well as strong community ties; and the sponsorship of extension or continuing-education courses and other events in off-campus locations convenient to those whose homes or jobs are remote from the regular classrooms.

(8) The alumni, especially those who live near the campus, should be involved more extensively in nonathletic university activities and programs. In many cases, the internal constituencies have either assumed alumni did not care about anything more than the football team's record and prospects, or have simply been too busy with internal problems to do more than arrange an occasional meeting at which the president would speak. Recently, these stereotypes have been drawn into question. Reports of alumni committees at both Columbia and CCNY in the spring of 1970 concentrated not upon athletic policy but, surprisingly, on the vital and central academic and governance issues. The substantive conclusions and recommendations of both reports read far more like the views of radical students than of prototype "old blues." The creation of universitywide deliberative bodies has involved graduates in new ways; Columbia's senate, for example, sets aside several seats for alumni representatives and thus affords alumni limited access to major university decisions. Transformations of governing boards have also given alumni a new stake in governance. Many institutions have just appointed recent graduates as trustees; in several states, young alumni have been added to the governing board, either by legislation or by gubernatorial initiative. Stanford has perhaps gone farthest in this respect; the board has been enlarged by the addition of eight alumni trustees in the fall of 1970. Four of these are elected from among graduates under the age of thirty-five; hence one eighth of the board now speaks directly for the young graduates.

Recent changes suggest there may be independent value in the involvement of alumni in a far wider range of university activities and decisions. Where the focus is upon community relations or ties between the internal and external worlds of the university, special benefits may be realized. Here, as in other areas where we have suggested greater community consciousness and a sharing of governance, the addition of a new voice need not impair or dilute the participation of the internal campus constituencies. What is true for the community is also true for the alumni: The better informed its spokesmen are, the greater the likelihood of tolerance and understanding in time of crisis. Thus, paradoxically, giving up a bit of autonomy may turn out to be the wisest means of protecting it.

(9) In return, the university should ask more of the community—not so much to be left alone as to be allowed to be the different, often unorthodox, and sometimes threatening institution it must be if free inquiry and scholarship are to flourish. Much of the tension and hostility toward universities results from basic misunderstanding by its neighbors of the important ways in which a university differs from a high school, a summer camp, a YMCA or other superficially similar institutions populated largely by young people. Until the community better understands how and why a university differs from these other entities, mayors and city councils will continue to treat them alike. Yet scholarship, inquiry, and research cannot flourish in an institution surrounded by the external constraints characteristic of a high school or a camp or a youth hostel. The process of differentiation is as arduous as it is essential for the future of academic freedom in the United States. Universities have been largely derelict in initiating that process. That the surrounding community continues to harbor misconception, truncated perception, and narrow suspicion about academic life is in some measure the fault of the universities themselves—their presidents, their governing boards, their faculties, and their students. The community cannot understand any more about an institution than they are given to know. Yet, if the events of May 1970 teach one clear lesson, it is that the process of mutual understanding and education must commence at once.

A

CHRONOLOGIES
OF THE EVENTS

Kent Chronology

Thursday April 30, 1970

Evening. Over nationwide television, President Richard Nixon
   announces his decision to send active combat forces into
   Cambodia.

Friday May 1, 1970

11:00 PM   Students begin jeering at passing cars on Water Street,
   the location of bars and taverns frequented by students. The

   The chronologies of the events leading up to and including the
killings at Kent State University and Jackson State College are taken
essentially from the account set down in the Scranton Report.

99

street is effectively closed off, and a bonfire is started in the center. Trashing occurs and store windows are broken.

12:30 AM   Mayor Leroy Satrom closes the bars on Water Street, and city police and sheriff's officers move in to clear the streets.

12:47 AM   Mayor Satrom phones the governor's office in Columbus and reports to the administrative assistant his belief that the SDS has taken over part of Kent. The Ohio Adjutant General, Sylvester Del Corso sends a National Guard liaison officer to assess the situation.

1:00 AM   Students are driven from the downtown area back to the campus by Kent city police and county deputies using tear gas. A freak accident near campus draws the attention of the students and the crowd drifts away near the entrance to the campus.

Saturday May 2, 1970

Morning   Mayor Satrom bans the sale of liquor, firearms, and gas not pumped directly into the car in the city of Kent. He also establishes an 8:00 PM to 6:00 AM curfew for the city but a 11:00 PM to 6:00 AM curfew for the campus. The students, however, are told about the 8:00 curfew, not the later hour.

1:00 PM   Lieutenant Charles Barnette of the National Guard informs university officials that if the national guard were called, it "would assume complete control of the entire area."

5:00 PM   A meeting is held between Satrom, Barnette, and campus officials (President Robert I. White is out of town). The mayor decides that the National Guard is necessary, but campus officials leave the meeting with the belief that the guard will only be used in the town of Kent, not on the campus.

7:30 PM   A crowd of students on campus grows to about two thousand and gathers in front of the ROTC building. They begin to throw rocks and make about a dozen attempts to ignite the building.

9:00 PM   The fire truck arrives, only to have its hoses slashed and rocks thrown at the firemen who withdraw. As the live ammunition inside the ROTC building begins to explode, the campus police arrive and attempt to disperse the crowd with tear gas.

9:30 PM   National Guard Generals Del Corso and Canterbury arrive in Kent at Satrom's request. The Guard has preceded them. After consultation with the mayor, one unit is dispatched to prevent students from entering the downtown area. Another unit is sent to protect the retreating firemen. A small shed near the campus tennis courts is set afire. The blaze is extinguished by students.

11:55 PM   The National Guard has cleared the campus with tear gas. General Canterbury reports the situation is under control.

Sunday May 3, 1970

10:00 AM   Governor James A. Rhodes arrives and holds a news conference. He indicates that every force of law available will be used to "eradicate the problems. We are not going to treat the symptoms."

A leaflet is distributed indicating curfew hours and banning all rallies. President White, having returned to Kent, issues a statement saying events have taken decisions out of university hands.

9:00 PM   A crowd gathers on the commons and is told to disperse. An announcement is made that the curfew has been changed from 1:00 a.m. to immediately. The crowd is dispersed with tear gas, but part reassemble at one of the university gates. They are told, falsely, that President White and Mayor Satrom will speak to them. One university official later indicated he had told the student who made the announcement that President White would not be present.

11:00 PM   Police are told that the two officials will not speak to the students, and it is announced to the crowd. Colonel Harold Finley announces that the curfew is in effect immediately and the students begin verbal abuse, and then throw rocks. Tear gas is returned, and two students receive minor cuts from bayonets. Three guardsmen are bruised and cut by rocks.

After 11:00 PM Some students are chased across campus with tear gas and into the library, which is locked after them. They are later allowed to leave. Fifty-one arrests are made that evening.

11:40 PM General Canterbury returns, but finds the campus quiet.

Monday May 4, 1970

10:00 AM Canterbury calls a meeting, attended by Mayor Satrom, Major Donald E. Manly of the Ohio State Highway Patrol, Major William R. Shimp of the Nat'l Guard and the Kent City Safety Director. Discussion centers around a student rally planned for the noon hour. There is general agreement that the rally is to be cancelled.

11:00 AM Students begin gathering on the commons. Some come to see if a rally will be held, some come out of curiosity, some come to protest the National Guard's presence on campus. Three National Guard units line up on the commons shortly before noon. The guardsmen have had an average of three hours sleep, having been on duty most of the night. They are armed with loaded M-1 rifles.

11:30 AM Canterbury arrives with Lieutenant Colonel Charles R. Fassinger of the National Guard. By 11:45, some five hundred students are on the campus, and Canterbury calls for them to disperse.

11:50 AM A Kent State policeman drives around the crowd in a jeep, ordering the crowd to disperse. He is cursed, shouted at, and stoned.

11:58 AM Canterbury orders the ninety-six men and officers under his command to form a skirmish line, shoulder to shoulder and move across the campus toward the students. Each man's rifle is loaded and locked in the "ready" position.

102

Eight to ten gas cannisters are fired into the crowd, which begins to scatter.

The guardsmen, bayonets fixed and gas masks in place, are ordered to march across the flat commons, scattering students before them up a steep hill. Guardsmen are pelted with rocks as they top the hill and march down to a practice field.

12:10 PM   After about ten minutes, Canterbury concludes that his dispersal order has been accomplished and orders the troops back up the hill in the direction they had just come. He erroneously believes they have exhausted their gas supply.

In the wake of this "retreat," some students become more aggressive and approach closer, although the intensity of rock throwing has diminished. As the guard marches up the hill, the students thereon pass to let them through. A small group of about twenty-five to fifty at the top of the hill retreat. However, as the guardsmen near the top of the hill, a group of students surges toward them, the leading edge of which approaches no more than twenty yards, the mass of which is sixty or seventy-five yards from the Guard.

As they reach the top of the hill, the Guard turns. One shot is fired and then a volley of M-1 fire. Sixty-one shots are fired in about thirteen seconds. Four persons lie dying and nine are wounded.

At first, many students believe that blanks have been fired. As they realize the truth, they react with anger, screaming at the Guard. Ambulances are called, and students link arms, forming rings around bodies to keep them from further injury.

About an hour after the shooting, the commons and hills around are clear. Members of the faculty have been instrumental in calming students and preventing further confrontation.

President White, at lunch at the time of the shootings, is informed and returns immediately to the campus. He orders the campus closed for the rest of the week. In the meantime,

Robert M. O'Neil

Portage County Prosecutor Ronald T. Kane has obtained a temporary injunction to close the campus. The campus does not reopen until the summer session, more than five weeks later.

Jackson Chronology

There was no apparent connection between the two campus tragedies. The student disturbances which occurred for two days on the Jackson campus prior to the shootings were not seemingly political in nature and, in fact, were initially characterized by the president of the college as the "annual spring riots." A chronology of the events can best be understood with the following geographic features of the Jackson campus in mind.

The campus is bisected by Lynch Street. Lynch Street is a major commuter thoroughfare, carrying a heavy load of traffic into the city of Jackson. It runs east and west through the heart of the campus. Stewart Hall, a men's dormitory, faces onto Lynch at a point approximately in the middle of the campus. Alexander Hall, the women's dormitory and scene of the shootings, is about two blocks east of Stewart and about a block west of the point where Lynch Street enters the campus.

May 13, 1970

Dusk until midnight   Students and corner boys throw rocks back and forth across Lynch Street at white motorists. The reason for the rock-throwing is not determined.

10:00 PM   Lynch Street is closed off by Jackson city police.

10:15 PM   A curfew of 10:30 PM is announced. No effort is made to enforce it.

10:30 PM   A campus security officer, driving on Lynch Street, is bombarded with rocks as he passes Stewart Hall. He is not injured. Two trash trailers are pulled onto Lynch Street and set afire.

10:45 PM   About one hundred youths are dispersed from the area in front of the ROTC building. They leave after hearing

104

pleas from Dean of Men Edward Curtis, Security Officer M. P. Stringer and campus student leaders.

10:50 PM Jackson city police and a unit of the Mississippi Highway Patrol with "Thompson's tank" (an armored vehicle equipped to dispense tear gas and used only on campus) move onto campus and around the ROTC building.

12:15 AM Jackson city police move away from the ROTC building via the edge of campus (to avoid a confrontation by passing through the center). They take up a position on Lynch Street to prevent crowds from moving downtown. A conference is held among Mayor Russell Davis, Chief of Police M. B. Pierce and Lieutenant Warren Magee of the police squad. They decide that the police will not return to the campus proper.

May 14, 1970

3:00 AM The adjutant general of Mississippi, Major General Walter Johnson informs President John A. Peoples that the National Guard is on the alert and warns that tear gas will be used in case of trouble.

2:30 PM Dr. Peoples informs student leaders that the National Guard is being mobilized.

Dusk Despite Dr. Peoples' request to Chief Pierce to close Lynch Street at dusk (a procedure previously used in times of disturbance), barricades are removed and the street is opened to traffic.

9:30 PM Small groups in front of Stewart Hall throw rocks at passing motorists. Lynch Street is closed.

10:00 PM An unidentified black man announces to a crowd of about two hundred that Charles Evers (brother of slain civil rights leader Medger Evers) and his wife have been killed. This same false rumor is spread by telephone to several bars on the edge of campus.

11:00 PM General Johnson puts the Guard into positions on Lynch Street near both ends of campus. Meanwhile, the police radio announces that a dump truck has been moved

105

by students in front of Stewart Hall and the front seat set afire. A nonstudent fires a handgun at the gas tank. Chief of Police Pierce orders Lieutenant McGee to take twenty-six men and Thompson's tank and clear the streets on campus. The police and forty highway patrolmen who joined them move onto campus and take a position between Stewart Hall and the burning truck. While waiting for the fire truck, they report being fired upon. Rocks and pieces of brick are thrown by the increasingly large crowd in front of Stewart, but no serious injuries are reported by firemen or police. A patrolman fires a shotgun blast into a fourth story window (ostensibly thinking he saw a sniper) but no one is hit.

After 11:00 PM   Firemen proceeding to the other side of campus to put out a bonfire report hearing small arms fire. (The bonfire is on the eastern end of campus, about a block past Alexander Hall.) The city and state police, led by Thompson's tank, move east from Stewart Hall. Meanwhile, the National Guard and the mayor move east toward Stewart Hall, about three blocks behind the police. The tank and police line up before Alexander Hall, the U-shaped women's dormitory. (The two "ends" of the U front on Lynch Street.) The crowd is shouting taunts at the police. Rocks are thrown, and orders to disperse are given. Some bystanders say the dispersal orders cannot be heard over the jeers. A TV cameraman claims to have heard a shot, followed by some shots from the officers near him. Suddenly, a general barrage of gunfire issues from the officers. Most of the firing is directed at one wing of the women's dormitory. However, neither of the two people killed is in the dormitory, nor in the line of fire between the dormitory and the police. Several students are wounded, some inside the dormitory. The barrage, taped by a reporter, lasts 28 seconds. General Johnson arrives from Stewart Hall and asks who gave the order to fire. He is told, "No one."

B

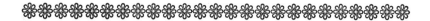

EXCERPTS
FROM THE SPECIAL
COMMITTEE REPORT

The foreword was written by the Past Presidents' Committee of the Kent AAUP.

Early in its investigation, the Special Committee that prepared this Report became the subject of controversy when its motives and methods were called publicly to question. At the suggestion of the Chairman of the Special Committee, the Executive Committee of the AAUP authorized the President to appoint two ad hoc committees: one, the Standby Committee, to hear new testimony; the

Prepared by the Kent State Chapter of the American Association of University Professors, Winter 1969–1970.

other, the Past Presidents' Committee, to comment on the report of the Special Committee. Whatever the circumstances that gave us this opportunity, we welcome it.

We are persuaded that the careful reader will find this Report to be the work of a group of dedicated scholars who have honestly, even bravely, tried to make sense of a bewilderingly complex series of events. If the reader feels that the Special Committee has expected an unusually high degree of wisdom and perfection on the part of the Administration in its handling of the crises, it is fair to remark that the reader is quite likely to bring the same high standards to bear on the Report itself. We are aware, because of having been close to the project, that it was finished under the extreme press of time. Even so, its merits are manifest. The Special Committee, like the Administration, the faculty, and the student body, is made up of fallible human beings who have found themselves facing an unprecedented situation triggered by a group of students whose disillusionment with their society and their government has led them to embrace the dangerous doctrine that the end justifies the means. Obviously, no university has yet found a fully satisfactory way of dealing with the explosive problems that have turned the ivy tower into an embattled fortress rent by internecine warfare. The Vietnam war goes on; poverty and racism thrive; and the humanist's dream has become very like a nightmare. Caught in the middle is the man who is chiefly responsible for the University, its President, and pressed against his temple is the muzzle of a long shotgun that reaches to the State Capitol. We believe we speak for the Special Committee as well as for ourselves when we say that the President deserves our sympathy and understanding.

This study documents a few deliberate provocations, a few deliberate lies, and many errors of judgment and sins of omission. But above all, it clearly implicates and indicts every possible element of the University community—even including the AAUP which initiated and carried out this investigation—in the exacerbation of an already deteriorating situation. On the other hand it calls attention to one of the most singular aspects of the whole affair: *the fact that no blood was shed*. We join with the Special Committee in commending President White and his Administration on the foresight and good sense they showed in their plans for avoiding that kind of violent overreaction that has stained other campuses. The University Police, as the Report reminds us, demonstrated remarkable restraint during the incident at the Administration Building. The AAUP has in the past been critical of the University Police, and it is a pleasure to congratulate them now.

In a university, learning is paramount. We feel that some of the principal *educational* conclusions to be drawn from this Report are the following:

> (1) *At the heart of democracy, which is "ruled" by the majority, there must be a leaning over backward to protect the political rights of individuals and minority groups: in particular the freedom of speech, of dissent, of assembly, to petition for redress of grievances, and the right of due process. Among other things, the treatment of CCC recorded in the Report indicates that there are many persons who lack appreciation of the democratic process.*
>
> *In this regard it is not enough that the law is properly applied to any individual or group. In addition we must not single out any one to whom or against whom the law is applied and allow others to go scot free. Such duplicity constitutes political repression just as well as other forms of demagoguery.* (2) *At the base of an academic community should be a dedication to truth and objectivity. The shameful and deliberate disregard of truth recorded here indicates a need on the part of many for a rededication to ideals. This includes also the necessity of refraining from deliberate untruths and of retracting and apologizing for those falsifications which are passed on unknowingly and later found to be untrue.* (3) *In frantic anxiety to maintain the body politic and "preserve law and order" we may do such vital damage to that body that it may end up a mere vegetable. "At what long-term cost were certain evils avoided? . . . Is violence to facts . . . less to be avoided than physical violence? . . . The University—our*

109

whole society—is today being tested by those who may themselves fail every test. Their failure, however, provides little consolation if in the heat of the trial we preserve our authority by departing from the principles that render that authority proper and just." It is possible to win all the battles and lose the war. It is possible to preserve law and order and have our institution end up being a nonuniversity. This Report will, hopefully, aid us in avoiding this catastrophe. (4) The confusions and difficulties arising from the spread of rumors are abundantly set forth in this Report. We recommend the creation of a rumor-control center, even though this may take money from other enterprises of the University. (5) The investigation disclosed here points out the necessity of an organization on campus which stands outside the legal organization and which we can use to act as gadfly and watchdog for ourselves. The AAUP has served that function elsewhere as well as here, even though it too has been found wanting. Like other elements of the University community, it can learn from this document.

Kent State University is first and foremost an educational institution for which teaching, learning, and the advancement of knowledge constitute its sole reasons for being. If we fail to use this remarkable document for educational purposes, if we fail to learn from it, then we shall have failed miserably. At the time of the crisis last spring, feelings were high. For some they are still high. And in many cases perhaps rightfully so. But if the material in this Report is used for smearing or for sensationalism or for reiterating "I told you so," then the tremendous outlay of energy and time and thought that has gone into it has been wasted. For the Special Committee's purpose has not been one of fault-finding. Rather, its purpose has been educational.

Dwight Arnold
William Hildebrand
Thomas Myers

No Heroes, No Villains

The first part of the report dealt with the incident in the spring of 1969 at the Music and Speech Building. The conclusions are set forth here.

It is unquestionably true that members of SDS . . . engaged in irresponsible and criminal acts. In the Committee's view the University had no choice other than to undertake disciplinary or punitive action against those participating in these acts.

Whether the calling of "outside police" should have been part of that action, however, is more questionable. The Kent City Police, the County Police, and the State Highway Patrol have traditionally been regarded as "outside police," and their use on university campuses, at least until the past several years, has been rare. Which administrative officer of the University called which police unit at what particular time and for what reason have not been ascertained. We have the testimony of Vice President Matson that the police were called to deal with a volatile situation at the rear entrance of the Music and Speech Building, where there were scuffles and minor fist-fighting.

It would appear, however, that at some point a decision was taken to pursue mass arrests of students disrupting disciplinary hearings. Once this decision was made, it followed by prearrangement that the mass arrests would be conducted by the State Highway Patrol because of their superior discipline and skill. The accounts of all witnesses confirm that the police forces present behaved, in a tense situation, not merely properly, but well.

But the decision to call for "outside police" was taken without consultation with representatives of the faculty. Yet such a decision is of the greatest import, insofar as it departs from the tradition whereby the campus is a kind of sanctuary. The tradition of sanctuary does not mean that acts that would be illegal if committed off campus should enjoy legitimacy and legality on campus. Rather it refers to the essence of the academic community as a place where reason, truth, and dialogue enjoy free play. Where police are to be called onto the campus, it seems to us there should be genuine consultation with representative elements of the *entire faculty*. To those who may argue that time does not permit such consultation, we offer the democrat's traditional answer: "The great impediment to action is, in our opinion, not discussion, but the want of that knowledge which is gained by discussion preparatory to action."

The Committee's view, which is in general agreement with the resolutions adopted at the national meeting of the AAUP in May 1969,[1] is that "outside police" should not be called in except when both of the following conditions are present: (1) the University Police are incapable of dealing with the emergency; (2) either there is clear and present danger to persons or to property, or injury to persons or damage to property has already been inflicted.

While our judgment is admittedly after the fact, we are not now convinced that both these conditions prevailed at the Music and Speech Building on April 16. Though glass was broken in one door and another was broken open, no effort appears to have been made by students to seize the building; no research files were destroyed or in danger of destruction; no classes were disrupted. We regret that consultative procedures were not observed. There appeared to be ample consultations on other questions during the series of events surrounding the Music and Speech incident, particularly on having the faculty speak in the dormitories about the CCC rally.

The second section of the report dealt with the university administration's policy regarding suspension of students involved in

[1] "Academic due process, both procedural and substantive, must be guaranteed. Should the maintenance of academic order prove a task beyond the powers of regularly constituted institutional organs, and should it prove unhappily necessary to resort to the civil power, decisions as to its use should be made in the first instance by responsible administrative officers and faculty members in the service of academic criteria and not of political expediency. . . . Having affirmed that the initiative in that protection must rest with properly constituted academic authorities, the Annual Meeting states its conviction that the present tragic season in our intellectual life must not be made the occasion for premature or punitive intervention by public officials or law enforcement officers." *AAUP Bulletin,* 1969, *55*(2), 152.

disorder—the so-called immediate suspension policy. A brief portion of the committee's conclusions concerning the validity of the policy is reprinted here.

We conclude that the Administration acted within its legal powers in promulgating the immediate suspension policy, but we find serious questions on two fronts: (1) whether a proper and adequate notification was made to the University community and (2) whether a proper and necessary participation by that community was sought in evolving the policy. In connection with the first question, if notification does not meet the specifications set forth earlier, then legal due process was not shown students in the application of the policy; but this would be a matter for the courts to decide. In connection with the second question, if the University community was not properly involved in the evolution of the policy, then, regardless of whether *legal* due process was observed, what we might call *academic* due process was infringed upon. Let us deal with each in turn. Regarding proper notification consider the following points:

(1) The *FYI* Weekly News Potpourris of March 16 and 30 were sent to student leaders but not to the student body at large. Consequently publication cannot have occurred therein in accordance with the requirements of due process. For Section 3345.21 of the Ohio Code Supplement is quite definite on this point. The relevant regulation "shall be published in a manner reasonably designed to come to the attention of, and be available to, *all* . . . students" (emphasis added).

(2) The March 7 issue of the [Daily Kent] *Stater* contains only one sentence concerning *immediate* suspension. And that sentence is not part of the immediate suspension policy statement prepared by Vice President Matson, nor does it mention that policy statement or Vice President Matson by name, nor does it state any *specific* kind of behavior with respect to which the penalty may be imposed. The sentence expresses no rule of conduct and therefore, *a fortiori*, none that can be violated. Moreover, in Vice President Matson's statement reported in the March 28 *Stater*, he speaks of

113

implementing the procedures outlined in "the [March 7] report." In the March 7 *Stater,* however, no "report" is named or otherwise uniquely specified, nor is any quoted or quoted from. Consequently publication cannot have occurred in that issue in accordance with the requirements of due process.

(3) The headline of the March 28 *Stater* is also the lead of the article in which the other alleged publication of the immediate suspension policy occurred. That headline is, "Fee Hike Due for Out-of-State Students," which surely is not likely to call anyone's attention to a new conduct regulation. Moreover, in the article, President White's and Vice President Matson's relevant statements each take a paragraph or less, near the middle of a twenty-three paragraph article concerning entirely unrelated matter. In short, with respect to the full article, their statements are easily overlooked and, even if read, are not likely to get the recognition their alleged import warrants. Finally, President White's "We *are establishing* procedures for immediate suspension in times of mass disruptions" (emphasis added) implies that there were not yet any procedures when he spoke.

With regard to the first question, then, we are forced to conclude that the notification made to students failed to satisfy the requirements of the Ohio Code as well as the observances of the U.S. Court of Appeals. . . .

Turning to the second question raised above, we are able to discern no way in which the University community was properly included in the evolution of the immediate suspension policy. Professor John Beacom, who chaired the ad hoc Student-Faculty Committee which, after long study and effort, brought forth what subsequently became the Student Conduct Code, reports that he was in no manner consulted about this most critical amendment of procedures which are, presumably, supplemental to that Code. The Student and Faculty senates were both bodies that had passed on the Student Conduct Code, but neither body was advised or consulted regarding the evolution and character of this most significant supplement. It is without doubt that this failure of the Administration to effect meaningful participation by the University community is the singly most aggravating factor in the whole affair, particularly for faculty, but perhaps no less so for students.

Vice President Matson indicated that the pressure of the times did not permit the long, tedious review which referring the matter to faculty and students would have entailed. The Ohio Code and the Board of Trustees had together set forth demands for immediate action which the immediate suspension policy sought to satisfy. Such contentions, of course, are debatable, the issue revolving around what is considered immediate and relevant action. The submission of the need for a supplemental policy, embodying, perhaps, immediate suspension of certain classes of offenders, to a committee such as Professor Beacom's and/or to the Student and Faculty senates could have been construed as just such an immediate and relevant action.

However, if it was and continued to be the judgment of the Administration and/or the Board of Trustees that a supplemental policy, like the immediate suspension policy, had to be instrumented post haste, then what was required to satisfy proper participation of faculty and students seems clear. The President should have announced the immediate suspension policy as a provisional or *pro tem* procedure. Simultaneously he should have made public that he was charging a joint committee of the Student and Faculty senates to study and evolve through their respective bodies an amendment to the Student Conduct Code that would ultimately replace the provisional policy and become the permanent procedure. Without doubt had some such effort been made meaningfully to involve the University community in this matter, much, if not all, of the grounds for indignant concern on the part of those not immediately involved in the April 16 affair would not have existed.

Due Process and the Application of the Policy

In the preceding section, we introduced the concept of *academic due process* in referring to the need to involve the academic community in decisions that are critical to it. Most of our previous discussion, however, was about due process in its legal sense. Let us

115

in this final section on immediate suspension deal with particulars related to the concept and application of due process in an academic setting.

The nature, methods, and procedures of academic due process are determined by the academic community's educational goals: the effective pursuit, discovery, communication, and rational criticism of putative truths. Any student who interferes with academic due process, either by violence or the threat of violence, thereby excludes himself from the academic community. And in so doing, he incurs whatever sanction is appropriate to his specific offense. Certainly the University's tolerance should not extend to its permitting violent action that hinders its realizing its objectives. Compatibility with the University's educational objectives is what is at issue here. . . .

Summarily, we find that there were the following violations of legal or academic due process in executing the immediate suspension policy:

(1) In direct violation of legal due process . . . and academic due process, Negro students were exempt from the application of the policy simply because they were Negroes.

(2) At least two policemen in charge of securing the Music and Speech Building against trespass gave contradictory directives to some students attempting to go to the third floor of the building, one policeman saying that entrance thereto was forbidden and the other saying that it was permissible.

(3) Some students who neither broke into nor trespassed upon the third floor of the Music and Speech Building, but who went there because they were curious to see what was happening, were not distinguished from those who did break into or trespass upon the third floor. A person is not trespassing upon a place ordinarily lawfully entered upon, if a policeman is present and does not attempt to dissuade him from entering upon it, but rather allows him freely to do so. Yet the immediate suspension policy was applied to students of both types.

(4) The provision of Item A-3 of the Code of Student

Conduct that requires advance written notification of formal disciplinary action was violated with respect to at least one student.

(5) Item B-1 of the Code of Student Conduct, concerning inquiry into the appropriateness of medical or counseling referral, was violated with respect to at least one student.

(6) Although one student's disciplinary hearing was held on April 22, 1969, and although the letter informing her of the charges against her was dated April 18, 1969, the envelope bearing the letter was postmarked April 21, 1969, indicating that she was not in fact given sufficient time to prepare her case adequately.

(7) At the same student's hearing, Mr. Oates [the University official who presented charges] tried to pressure members who were hearing the case into finding the student guilty and went so far as to attempt to prevent one of them from asking questions of a testifying policeman.

(8) At that same student's hearing, Mr. Oates both prosecuted the case against her and instructed the Judiciary Board that was judging it.

(9) At that same student's hearing, Mr. Oates failed to explain their duties to the members of the Judiciary Board that was hearing it.

(10) Mr. Marshall assumed three different roles in conducting each of several disciplinary hearings, complainant, recording secretary, and witness to and commentator upon deliberations of the judges.

Conclusion

We conclude that in the application of the policy and the treatment of those whose conduct appeared in contravention of it, the University failed on numerous counts to satisfy both legal and academic due process. We believe that the policy, even in its fullest form rendered to date, does not make adequate provisions for the rights that have been made clear in section iii. Moreover, as indicated in section ii, the logically prior and fundamental right of

117

members of the University community to participate in the evolution of its crucial rules, values, and policies has not been observed.

The final section of the report was addressed to the hearings held in April 1969 before the Student-Faculty Judiciary Board concerning charges against the suspended students. The committee reviewed the board's jurisdiction, role, and operation in considerable detail. Only the conclusions appear here.

One effect of the mass suspensions of April 16 was the burden they placed upon the Student-Faculty Judiciary Board. This body is "the court of original jurisdiction for all disciplinary cases in which the sanction could be disciplinary suspension or disciplinary dismissal from the University" (*Student Handbook*). The membership consists of two faculty members, two students, and a Dean of the defendant's College or a faculty member designated by that Dean. Normally this permanent board and another alternate one are able to carry the load of disciplinary cases, but in emergencies the Student Conduct Code allows for the setting up of special *ad hoc* committees to help in the work.

The Code of Student Conduct states that these hearings are not court hearings. "It is to be recognized," the Code says, "that a university cannot fully assure a hearing of a judicial nature . . ." Nevertheless, it continues,

> *no formal disciplinary action (namely, that which could result in the imposition of a probation, suspension, or dismissal) shall be taken by or in the name of the University unless the student has been informed in writing of the charges against him and has been offered the opportunity to appear alone or with any other person or persons to advise, assist, or act as counsel(s) before the appropriate committee, board, court or official; to know the nature and source of the evidence against him and to cross-examine witnesses against him; to present evidence, including witnesses on his own behalf; and been informed of appropriate appeal routes.*

Dean Matson and members of the student personnel staff, in their testimonies before this Committee, emphasized that the hearings do not pretend to be strict legal hearings, but are confidential meetings between the members of the Board, the Dean, and the student. But however definite the procedure was outlined on paper and in official testimony, in actual practice the hearings were marked by considerable confusion. . . .

It is the conclusion of this Committee that the procedures of the Student-Faculty Judiciary Board were not adequate to meet the new kinds of disciplinary cases brought before it after the April disruptions, and that now more effective procedures need to be developed to protect the rights of all concerned.

The committee's overall conclusions and recommendations were contained in the final pages of the report, which are reprinted in full here.

Mindful of the complexities in reporting and interpreting the events of last spring, we nevertheless offer these judgments based on the evidence we have gathered. We take note of the cooperation of faculty, students, and representatives of the Administration, some eighty of whom have given testimony, either voluntarily or by invitation, as to their perceptions of the events of last April. We regret that neither President Robert I. White nor Chief Security Officer Donald Schwartzmiller was available to testify before this Committee. Each could have added appreciably to our understanding of the rationale, goals, and tactics of the University in dealing with campus disruptions.

The reader who goes through the entire Report will find a great many conclusions which the Committee has drawn, among them the following: Legal due process was violated by the Administration's failure adequately to publish the rules regarding immediate suspension. Academic due process was violated by the Administration's failure to consult with faculty and students in the development of the immediate suspension policy. The decision to call outside police should not have been taken without consultation with the faculty. The calling of outside police involves a shift in control over disciplinary processes from University to civil authority and should be taken only after such consultation. While crisis situations may not always allow time for consultation before calling outside police, we believe that previous to the incidents of April 9 and 16 there was ample time for the Administration to develop, in cooperation with faculty and students, a procedural policy to be followed in crisis situations. The faculty, including the AAUP and the Faculty Senate, also is culpable on this point because of their failure to initiate such consultation.

Confusion and inadequacies were revealed in the student disciplinary procedures, particularly in the practice whereby the Administration spokesmen found themselves forced to play multiple roles: counselor, moderator, recording secretary, prosecutor, and judge. (It is only fair to note that the University did attempt to mitigate the consequences of the immediate suspensions—in empowering the Special Counsel to the President for Student Rights to lift certain suspensions—even though the process used here was *ad hoc* and confused by the crisis situation.) There were failures of student institutions and of individuals following the disruptions at the Music and Speech Building and the subsequent appearance of the CCC. We refer particularly to the succumbing by student-government leadership to rumor and, indeed, to its generating of rumor, and to the failure of the *Daily Kent Stater* to discharge its special obligations to the University community. The Office of Student Affairs discouraged efforts to establish open dialogue with the CCC and failed to deal equitably with that organization.

The thrust of this investigation has been to examine critically the reaction of Kent State University to crisis and challenge. We have not developed a detailed or balanced inquiry into the initiatives mounted by student groups, particularly SDS, with a view to presenting a broad-spectrum evaluation thereof. Such would have made impossibly long an already maximum effort by a faculty committee each of whose members had many other responsibilities. This choice of focus, however, does not, and indeed *should* not, be construed to imply that this Committee began or ended with

120

a favorable or even sympathetic opinion of student confrontation/ provocation politics. As it was, what information we developed about SDS showed it to be an often unreasonable and violent group whose members see no contradiction in mocking institutions from which they demand every right of due process.

It is also well to recognize in closing this Report that we seem to be venting, on the face of it, a note of criticism which contrasts discordantly with the widespread approval of and sense of gratitude toward an Administration that managed to avoid that brand of bitter, violent controversy given such unfavorable notice elsewhere. Physical conflict and injury would not merely have caused personal suffering and distress but, through the instant alert of television and radio, would have focused the attention of the entire nation on KSU with consequences and dire reverberations in many quarters. That this was avoided is not accidental and deserves the commendation of all.

On the other hand, it is fair to ask: At what long-term cost were certain immediate evils avoided? Did the University as an institution devoted to learning, communication, truth, and regard for the individual forfeit something vital to it in the exchange? Is violence to facts—and, we might say, to the vital principles in which we reside both as persons and as an institution—less to be avoided than physical violence? The rub is, of course, that the former violence is practiced free of physical suffering and with little or no immediate consequences in public outrage. Understandably an administrator forced to choose between actions resulting inevitably in one or the other will be sorely tempted to opt for that choice which preserves both the peace and his office while avoiding "the appearance of evil." It is up to us all to see to it that such choices, whether large or small, do not go unheeded, and, where wrong, unopposed. The University—our whole society—is today being tested by those who may themselves fail every test. Their failure, however, provides little consolation if in the heat of the trial we preserve our authority by departing from the principles that render that authority proper and just.

121

C

EXCERPTS FROM
THE PORTAGE COUNTY
GRAND JURY REPORT

VIII

Among other persons sharing responsibility for the tragic consequences of May 4, 1970, then, must be included the "twenty-three
concerned faculty of Kent State University," who composed and
made available for distribution on May 3, 1970, the following
document:

      Reprinted from *Higher Education and National Affairs,* Oct.
23, 1970, pp. 6–8.

No Heroes, No Villains

"The appearance of armed troops on the campus of Kent State University is an appalling sight. Occupation of the town and campus by National Guardsmen is testimony to the domination of irrationality in the policies of our government.

The President of the United States commits an illegal act of war and refers to his opposition as "bums." That students and faculty and, indeed, all thinking people reject his position is not only rational but patriotic. True, burning a building at Kent State University is no joke; we reject such tactics. Yet the burning of an ROTC building is no accident. We deplore this violence but we feel it must be viewed in the larger context of the daily burning of buildings and people by our government in Vietnam, Laos, and now Cambodia. Leadership must set the example if it is to persuade. There is only one course to follow if the people of this country—young and old—are to be convinced of the good faith of their leaders: The war must stop. The vendetta against the Black Panthers must stop. The Constitutional rights of all must be defended against any challenge, even from the Department of Justice itself. If Mr. Nixon instead continues his bankrupt, illegal course, the Congress must be called upon to impeach him.

Here and now we repudiate the inflammatory inaccuracies expressed by Governor Rhodes in his press conference today. We urge him to remove the troops from our campus. No problem can be solved so long as the campus is under martial law.

We call upon our public authorities to use their high offices to bring about greater understanding of the issues involved in and contributing to the burning of the ROTC building at Kent State University on Saturday, rather than to exploit this incident in a manner that can only inflame the public and increase the confusion among the members of the University community."

Signed by twenty-three concerned faculty
Kent State University,
Sunday afternoon, May 3, 1970

123

Robert M. O'Neil

Several hundred copies of this unusual document were distributed in the various dormitories situated on the Kent State University campus during the late afternoon and early evening of May 3, 1970. The offices and facilities of the Dean for the Faculty Council, known as the Ombudsman, were made available to those persons who participated in its preparation. If the purpose of the authors was simply to express their resentment to the presence of the National Guard on campus, their timing could not have been worse. If their purpose was to further inflame an already tense situation, then it surely must have enjoyed some measure of success. In either case, their action exhibited an irresponsible act clearly not in the best interests of Kent State University. Although twenty-three persons referred to at the close of the statement did not actually affix their signatures to the document, they, together with one additional party, did leave their signatures with the Dean for the Faculty Council as evidence of their authorship and approval.

It should be pointed out that at least sixty faculty members were invited to the meeting, but a majority apparently elected not to be associated with the product that resulted.

The conduct of these faculty members is in sharp contrast to those of the faculty who, through their efforts on May 4th, restored order and prevented further rioting after the shooting.

IX

We find that the major responsibility for the incidents occurring on the Kent State University campus on May 2nd., 3rd., and 4th. rests clearly with those persons who are charged with the administration of the University. To attempt to fix the sole blame for what happened during this period on the National Guard, the students or other participants would be inconceivable. The evidence presented to us has established that Kent State University was in such a state of disrepair that it was totally incapable of reacting to the situation in any effective manner. We believe that it resulted from policies formulated and carried out by the University over a

124

period of several years, the more obvious of which will be commented on here.

The administration at Kent State University has fostered an attitude of laxity, overindulgence, and permissiveness with its students and faculty to the extent that it can no longer regulate the activities of either and is particularly vulnerable to any pressure applied from radical elements within the student body or faculty. One example of this can be clearly seen in the delegation of disciplinary authority under a student conduct code which has proven totally ineffective. There has been no evidence presented to us that would indicate that college students are able to properly dispose of criminal offenders within their own ranks any more than they are capable of devising their own curriculum, participating in the selection of faculty, or setting the standards for their admission to or dismissal from the University. Neither have we been convinced that the faculty is necessarily equipped to assume and successfully carry out responsibilities of a purely administrative character which for many years were considered to be totally outside the area of responsibility normally associated with the teaching faculty of our colleges and universities. In short, a segment of the student population and the faculty have demanded more and more control of the administrative functions of Kent State University. The administrative staff has constantly yielded to these demands to the extent that it no longer runs the University.

The student conduct code, as already indicated, has been a total failure. As a matter of policy, all criminal offenses uncovered by the University Police Department, except those which constitute felonies, were referred to judicial boards composed solely of students residing in the dormitory where the alleged offender resided. These students determined the guilt or innocence of the accused and prescribed the punishment. The end result has been, of course, that where any final disposition has been made at all it has consisted of recommended counseling or some other meaningless sanction.

Offenses for which suspension or dismissal from the University could be imposed were heard by the Student Faculty Judiciary Council. Membership consists of two faculty members, two

125

students, and a fifth member who shall be a Dean of the defendant's college or a faculty member designated by him. A total of only five students were dismissed for nonacademic reasons during the academic year 1969–70 out of a total enrollment of more than 21,000.

A second example of where the University has obviously contributed to the crisis it now faces is the overemphasis which it has placed and allowed to be placed on the right of dissent. Although we fully recognize that the right of dissent is a basic freedom to be cherished and protected, we cannot agree that the role of the University should be to continually foster a climate in which dissent becomes the order of the day to the exclusion of all normal behavior and expression.

We receive the impression that there are some persons connected with the University who believe and openly advocate that on has a duty rather than a right to dissent from traditionally accepted behavior and institutions of government. This is evident by the administrative staff in providing a forum and available facilities for every "radical group" that comes along and the "speakers" that they bring to the campus. It has been the policy of Kent State University to routinely grant official recognition to every group that makes application. The few conditions that have been imposed are meaningless and we have been unable to find a single instance where recognition has been refused. This is the procedure by which the Students for a Democratic Society, Young Socialist Alliance, Red Guard, Student Religious Liberals, and other groups who advocate violence and disruption were granted recognition. Provisional recognition is automatic upon filing. During the period that is required to process the application, the organization is permitted to the same use of the University facilities that it has when fully recognized. No distinction is made between ordinary student organizations whose objectives are related to legitimate activities on campus and the politically active organizations whose membership openly advocates revolution and anarchy. Once temporary or permanent recognition is granted, the organization may sponsor speakers from off campus and have the use of University facilities and equipment for that purpose. It was in this manner that Jerry Rubin was brought to the campus in April, 1970, by the Student Religious Liberals. The inflammatory speech given by Mr. Rubin was so interspersed with vulgarity and obscenity that it could not be reported by the local news media.

A further example of what we consider an overemphasis on dissent can be found in the classrooms of some members of the University faculty. The faculty members to whom we refer teach nothing but the negative side of our institutions of government and refuse to acknowledge that any positive good has resulted during the growth of our nation. They devote their entire class periods to urging their students to openly oppose our institutions of government even to the point where one student who dared to defend the American flag was ridiculed by his professor before his classmates.

We do not mean to suggest that these faculty members represent a majority of the faculty at Kent State University. To the contrary, we suspect that they form a small minority of the total faculty, but this does not mean that their presence should be ignored.

The most discouraging aspect of the University's role in the incidents which have been the subject of our investigation is that the administrative leadership has totally failed to benefit from past events. The same condescending attitude toward the small minority bent on disrupting the University that existed last May is still present. On Wednesday, October 7, 1970, the Youth International Party, more commonly known as the "Yippies," applied for and were granted permission from the University to use its auditorium. The request for use of the University facilities was granted in the customary routine manner with no apparent interest in the purpose of the gathering. The meeting was later billed as a "Yippie Open Smoker" and was attended by some 250 persons. The agenda consisted of several speakers who exhorted in the usual obscene rhetoric with the customary demands to free Bobby Seale, remove ROTC from campus, and to put an end to the Liquid Crystals Institute. In retrospect, no possible purpose could be attributed to the meeting except to disrupt the normal operation of the University.

On Sunday night, October 11, 1970, two appearances were

scheduled at the Memorial Gymnasium for a rock music group known as the "Jefferson Airplane." During the second performance and while the "Airplane" were doing their musical numbers, color slides were projected onto a screen behind the group consisting of psychedelic colors, scenes of the Ohio National Guard on Kent State campus, and scenes of the shooting on May 4th, complete with views of the bodies of the victims.

On October 12th, the "Yippies" scheduled a second meeting at the auditorium, which was supposed in some manner to relate to the activities of this Grand Jury. Again, on October 14, 1970, the same "Yippie" group scheduled a noon rally on the commons. Neither of these events attracted more than a handful of spectators, and this is to the credit of the student body. What disturbs us is that any such group of intellectual and social misfits should be afforded the opportunity to disrupt the affairs of a major university to the detriment of the vast majority of the students enrolled there.

Conclusion

The members of this Special Grand Jury find that all the conditions that led to the May tragedy still exist. It is apparent that an apathetic university community has allowed a vocal minority to seize control of the university campus. This will continue until such time as the citizens, university administration, faculty and students take a strong stand against the radical element bent on violence.

The time has come to detach from university society those who persist in violent behavior. Expel the troublemakers without fear or favor. Evict from the campus those persons bent on disorder.

This Grand Jury has in this report been critical of Kent State University, but let no one assume that we do not consider the University a valued part of our community. It is our hope that out of this chaos will emerge order and purpose. It is our belief that Kent State University has the capacity to become a greater university in the future.

D

STATEMENT OF
ROBERT I. WHITE

N̶o university in American history has been so battered as Kent State University these past several months. Faculty, staff, students and trustees have been subjected to rumors, threats, some sensationalized reporting, a constant series of investigations, ripping reports, bomb scares, and countless other campus tension-builders.

Nevertheless, Kent State is a far better university today than a year ago. Despite tragic aftermaths and myriad of problems, it is operating openly and freely with a growing morale by both

President White of Kent State University read this statement before the National Association of State Universities and Land-Grant Colleges on November 9, 1970. It was widely noted in the press, but the full text has not been printed elsewhere.

129

students and faculty. This is a triumph of stamina, common sense, and loyalty to K.S.U.

Of the many studies and reports of our tragedy, probably none was so disconcerting to the campus community as the essay report of the Special State Grand Jury. The report's indictment of the university, coupled with a court order forbidding witnesses to comment on the report, added further to campus tensions—at Kent and in the nation.

Last Tuesday in Cleveland, Federal Judge Ben C. Green eloquently placed the issues in perspective. In his decision permitting those who were witnesses to comment on the report, Judge Green said, and I quote, "The events which occurred at Kent State University in the spring of this year are a matter of national, social, political, and moral concern and debate. The [Portage County Court] order prevents not only the three hundred [witnesses] from speaking, but the rest of the world from hearing," end of quote.

I know not whether the rest of the world is waiting to hear, but I feel strongly that the grand jury report is simply a local manifestation of a national problem.

Every one of the charges brought against us by the local grand jury has been made generally over the nation. However, every large-scale study—from the Scranton report to that by a segment of the republican congressional delegation—has pointed to factors far beyond the control of any of the universities.

In my opinion, the grand jury report was inaccurate, disregarded clear evidence, and, if pursued in all its nuances, would eventually destroy not only Kent State but all major universities in America.

We know full well that the grand jury report was well received among the general public. On many occasions I have commented on the distressing polarization of views with regard to our, or any university, and the almost hopeless task of anyone who attempts to hold a balance against the rash extremists on either side. In the grand jury's analysis, I see a prime example of a brewing national disaster.

130

No Heroes, No Villains

In their essay report, ten grand jurors charged that the major responsibility for the May tragedy rested on the administration of the university. More particularly, they noted what they called "general permissiveness" reflected in the nature of speakers, inability to control "radical elements," too much shared responsibility with the faculty, ineffectiveness of the student conduct code, tolerance of rallies, and overemphasis on dissent.

Throughout the pages of the grand jury report my colleagues and I are severely criticized, but the direction of the findings transcends the Kent State University administration. In fact, the constitutional safeguards of American democracy are themselves under fire. Our judgments must not be parochial. We must view the policies of Kent State as they are intended to reflect the purpose and mission of all education and as a reflection of the democratic structure of our society.

Dissent and demonstration over the social and political problems which plague our nation are not unique to the campus of Kent State University. The angry voice of dissent can be heard both on and off the campus and in the cities both large and small. But dissent in a democratic society does pose unique problems.

Universities have traditionally advocated the free and full expression of varying views and are committed to the concept of true academic freedom, which, in the unanimous view of our faculty senate, includes academic responsibility. Because of this commitment to the full exercise of free thought and discussion, the university is particularly vulnerable to exploitation by the radical or an extreme.

The balance between the right of free speech and peaceful dissent is a delicate one. The right to dissent is not the right to destroy. The academic community is not to be considered a sanctuary for those who wish to disobey the laws. We hold no brief for lawbreakers or for disrupters. But neither is the academic community a place where ideas—are to be suppressed. The constitutional safeguards of the Bill of Rights and, in particular, the First Amendment rights of free speech, press and assembly are worthy of the utmost protection.

131

Robert M. O'Neil

The comments in the grand jury report about campus speakers are judicially naive as well as fundamentally unworkable and ultimately undesirable. In a real sense the report leads into a censorship of points of view going quite beyond constitutional limits.

There has been and is a grotesque generalization of all of today's young people. There are some immeasurably sophisticated, well-trained dedicated destroyers. There also are some spoiled ones. But there are very, very many indeed who have seen much wrong in today's life and will work at any length to correct these wrongs short of irresponsible or destructive actions. It is [upon] these young men and women that we rest our hopes for the future. We must be quite careful not to tar all students with the same brush.

We recognize the satanic alliance between the extremes of the left and the extremes of the right in an assault upon the free and independent university. The effect has been growing polarization. Action produces reaction, followed by overreaction, and increasingly endangering the university's ability to exist.

Society in general with its courts and numerous law-enforcement agencies, faces serious challenge from those who would protest against alleged injustices. Despite its legal mechanism and the personnel available, I would suggest that the solutions are even more difficult in the university setting. By the nature of their mission, universities are without jails, without elaborate legal and judicial systems, and without large forces of security and police personnel although these factors are rapidly changing.

This is not to say that universities are helpless or that their administrative and judicial procedures are not in need of review and repair. I simply point out that the problems are difficult and complex.

The administrative programs of Kent State University have undergone extensive review since last May. Since then, the administrative structure has been altered, the security forces have been strengthened and better trained, the faculty have reviewed their role and responsibilities within the institution, and students have made their commitment to nonviolence real and meaningful. The

132

very numerous changes were generally well publicized and that all were not visibly apparent is by design.

Before closing, I want to make clear my belief that the panel of citizens who served in the difficult role as grand jurors made every effort to review testimony, to study evidence, and to report honestly their findings. At the same time, we must recognize that their general report reflects a frightening misunderstanding of the role and mission of higher education in our society.

We are dedicated to the preservation of a free and open society. We must remain so dedicated if our democracy is to survive.

E

HAMMOND VS. BROWN DECISION

The case of Hammond vs. Brown *was the second lawsuit brought in the federal courts to stop the prosecution of the persons indicted by the special grand jury and to have the report of the grand jury destroyed. The suit was brought by a diverse group of plaintiffs. They based their claims on several federal civil rights laws which grant relief in the federal courts to individuals whose constitutional rights and liberties have been infringed by state-government action.*

The first excerpt deals with the claims advanced by the non-indicted plaintiffs. Particular attention is given to the claims of the group of faculty members who had drafted and distributed the declaration of the "faculty twenty-three" on May 3, 1970.

United States District Court for the Northern District of Ohio, civil case C70-998, Jan. 28, 1971.

134

The protected rights claimed to be violated are in substance that the twenty-three faculty members were given no notice of the charges against them prior to the issuance of the Report of the Special Grand Jury; that the Grand Jury did not provide the twenty-three with an opportunity to "confront and cross examine their accusers to determine the factual basis for charges against them or to present evidence in their own behalf."

Though the twenty-three faculty members did not sign the letter of May 3, 1970, and though the Special Grand Jury Report does not name them, it is apparent from the Report that the twenty-three faculty members comprise an identifiable class. The names of the signers are known to the University administration, the Report makes clear, and it is reasonably probable that the names are known to some other faculty members, at least.

By the quoted language of Part VIII, the Grand Jury Report charges these twenty-three identifiable members of the faculty with complicity for the "tragic consequences of May 4, 1970." The Grand Jury indirectly says that the twenty-three intended to "inflame an already tense situation." The Grand Jury directly charges them with "an irresponsible act." Yet, though critical and condemnatory, the charges stop short of accusing the twenty-three faculty members of either specific offenses or general criminal conduct.

It follows that there is no denial of their rights of Due Process of law as guaranteed by the Fifth and Fourteenth Amendments. Further, these charges do not deprive the twenty-three faculty members of their rights under the Sixth Amendment, made applicable to the states by the Fourteenth Amendment, "to be informed of the nature and cause of the accusation; to be confronted with the witness against [them]."

However, it is determined and declared that these charges, bordering on criminal accusations, against the twenty-three identifiable faculty members, made by the Special Grand Jury, a formal accusing body of Portage County, irreparably impair and injure the right of these twenty-three faculty members to their protected right of free expression, protected by the First Amendment made

135

applicable to the states by the Fourteenth Amendment. It is further found and declared that the charges in Part VIII, made under color of state law, deprive the plaintiff faculty members and other faculty members within the identifiable class of twenty-three of constitutional rights in violation of 42 U.S.C. § 1983 (1964).

The court went on to consider broader claims of Kent faculty members, not necessarily among the "twenty-three," that the criticism contained in the report chilled freedom of expression and inquiry and thus endangered academic freedom. The court reviewed the pertinent portions of the grand jury report at some length, then considered the constitutional issues.

The claimed violation of First Amendment rights violative of Due Process presents a different matter. Let us assume a member of the Kent State faculty reads the Grand Jury's criticism of "overemphasis on dissent . . . in the classrooms of some members of the University faculty" and the Report's comment that this dissent "becomes the order of the day to the exclusion of all normal behavior and expression." He may reasonably believe that people in the Kent community (university and city) who have read Parts VIII and IX of the Report may well think the Report may refer to him. People in the community may well believe that a particular faculty member is one of the "small minority of the total faculty" who depart from "all normal behavior and expression."

A Report of the Special Grand Jury, an official accusatory body of the community, that criticizes faculty members for "overemphasis on dissent," thus seeking to impose norms of "behavior and expression," restricts and interferes with the faculty members' exercise of protected expression. The record reveals that this is happening.

Impairment of First Amendment freedom of expression is directly resulting from the Special Grand Jury Report. This is disclosed by candid and credited testimony of members of the faculty who appeared as witnesses. Because of the Report, instructors have altered or dropped course materials for fear of classroom controversy. For example, an assistant professor of English, after reading the Report, "scratched three poems" from her outline in her Introduction to Poetry course. The poems are "Politics" by William Butler Yeats, "Prometheus" by Lord Byron, and "Dover Beach" by Matthew Arnold.

In "Politics," Yeats writes: "And maybe what they say is true of war and war's alarms."

A university professor may add or subtract course content for different reasons. But when a university professor is fearful that "war's alarm," a poet's concern, may produce "inflammatory discussion" in a poetry class, it is evident that the Report's riptide is washing away protected expression on the Kent campus.

Other evidence cumulatively shows that this teacher's reaction was not isolated. The Report is dulling clasroom discussion and is upsetting the teaching atmosphere. This effect was described by other faculty witnesses. When thought is controlled, or appears to be controlled, when pedagogues and pupils shrink from free inquiry at a state university because of a report of a resident Grand Jury, then academic freedom of expression is impermissibly impaired. This will curb conditions essential to fulfillment of the university's learning purposes.

Finally, the court considered arguments of the plaintiffs that the indictments should be quashed since the grand jury had acted in bad faith.

The exclusive power to indict or not to indict is constitutionally and historically vested in a grand jury. Selective enforcement amounting to bad faith, therefore, cannot be inferred solely from the fact that the Grand Jury has indicted twenty-five persons in connection with the events at Kent State University and in Kent, Ohio, from May 1 through May 4, 1970; and that it did not indict any of the National Guardsmen. . . .

After considering all aspects of the claim of bad faith prosecution of the indictments amounting to a deprivation of the right to fair trial, it is determined and declared, on this record and at this pretrial stage of the state prosecutions, that a deprivation of the right to a fair trial has not been shown. Moreover, other than the continued official existence of the Report, there is no showing of facts that clearly prove an irreparable and immediate injury to the right to a fair trial. The first essential to the requested injunction against the Portage County Common Pleas Court prosecutions of the indictment is not established.

F

EXCERPTS FROM
THE ANALYSIS OF THE
OHIO GRAND JURY
REPORT

The manner in which the Grand Jury singles out the statement of "twenty-three concerned faculty" for lengthy quotation and criticism raises serious questions about both the competence and the intentions of the Grand Jury. Why is this statement, made by a very small group of faculty, singled out as particularly inflammatory while an earlier statement by the Governor of Ohio, to which these

Prepared for the Kent State University Faculty Senate by an ad hoc committee.

139

faculty members were in large measure responding, is not even mentioned (except in text of the quoted faculty statement itself)? Certainly the governor's statement, which achieved far wider distribution than that issued by the faculty group, and which accused the troublemakers of being "worse than the brown shirts and the communist element . . . the worst type of people that we harbor in America," (Scranton Commission report, pp. 35–36), must be considered as inflammatory as the statement attacked as "irresponsible" by the Grand Jury. The Grand Jury further declares that the timing of this "unusual" statement "could not have been worse," although, given the declared purpose of those who issued it, namely, to protest the presence of the national guard on the campus and urge its withdrawal, it would appear that the Jury is thereby suggesting that such protests and demands should not be issued at all.

It is particularly noteworthy that the Report implies that the meeting at which this statement was drawn up was called primarily or even solely for that purpose in spite of the fact that it had heard testimony from Dean Harold Kitner that this was not the case. Those who gathered on that Sunday afternoon have repeatedly indicated they were desperately trying to play a constructive role in what they accurately perceived to be a rapidly deteriorating situation. Their principal efforts were directed toward the convening of an immediate meeting of the entire faculty to deal with the crisis. (See Dean Kitner's press release of November 6, 1970.) The events of the following day only proved how justified their concern had been.

Finally, the Report indicates that the Grand Jurors either were not aware of, or did not want to publicize, the fact that some of those who signed the statement were among those whom they praise for their constructive efforts on May 4. That the Grand Jurors chose to devote such a substantial part of their Report to what was clearly an event of any peripheral importance (mentioned only in passing and without criticism in the Scranton Commission report—pp. 39–40—and not mentioned at all in the Justice Department report) can only weaken the credibility of the Grand Jury Report.

No Heroes, No Villains

The Grand Jury finds that "The major responsibility for the incidents on the K.S.U. campus rests clearly with those persons charged with the administration of the University . . . that it resulted from policies formulated and carried out by the University over a period of several years." Since no member of the administration was under indictment or formally charged, such statements are wholly outside the Jury's jurisdiction and, if true, would have resulted in charges against those with the "major responsibility."

The Grand Jury again in the same view finds, "The administration at KSU has fostered an attitude of laxity, overindulgency, and permissiveness with its students and faculty to the extent that it can no longer regulate the activities of either." It fails to take into account that a university is no longer *in loco parentis,* that the courts have well defined that students also have civil liberties and constitutional rights which are stringently upheld.

For instance, the Grand Jury reports, "One example of this can clearly be seen in the delegation of disciplinary authority under a student conduct code which has proven totally ineffective."

It further goes on to say, "There has been no evidence presented to us that would indicate that college students are able to properly dispose of criminal offenders within their own ranks." It is hardly surprising that no evidence was presented to them, as the purpose of the student code is not to dispose of criminal offenders, but for breaches of university regulations. If such offense is also a criminal offense, then such sanction imposed by the code is over and above the sentence of a criminal court.

The Jury also finds itself an authority in criminal rehabilitation, finding "Where any final disposition has been made at all, it has consisted of recommended counseling *or some other meaningless sanction*" (emphasis added). It places its only emphasis on a small number of students nonacademically dismissed in the academic year, failing to take into account suspension for specified periods, probationary periods, academic failures due to nonattendance, and the withdrawals due to legal sanctions.

The Grand Jury also finds overemphasis on the right to dissent. It "recognizes the right to dissent is a basic freedom to be

141

cherished and protected," but apparently finds difficulty in agreeing that those with political views different from its own should be allowed on campus and believes that speakers from such organizations should be banned from the campus. It finds categorically that "Students for a Democratic Society, Young Socialist Alliance, Red Guard, Student Religious Liberals, and other groups advocate violence and disruption," and unjustifiably draws a distinction between "legitimate activities on campus" and "politically active organizations."

The Jury, although acknowledging they are only a small minority, finds an overemphasis on dissent by faculty in the classrooms, finding members who "teach nothing but the negative side of our institution of government and refuse to acknowledge that any positive good has resulted during the growth of our nation. They devote their entire class periods to urging their students to openly oppose our institution." The Jurors fail to realize that competent professors often play the role of devil's advocate in a class in an attempt to stimulate thoughts and analysis over and above their beliefs.

In comparing this section with the other reports, we are struck with the fact that the Grand Jury Report is the only one which concludes the administration must be held primarily responsible for the tragic events. The Scranton Commission, in a general way, concludes that all groups have some lessons to learn but does not single out the administration. The length to which the Grand Jury Report goes to develop its case suggests the one-sided nature of its investigation.

Critical Issues Raised by the Report

In addition to the significant ways in which the Grand Jury Report is at variance with other investigative agencies, the Grand Jury Report is particularly disturbing because of the prejudice that it reveals and the unfortunate failure on the part of the Jury to understand how a university functions and what its goals are.

No Heroes, No Villains

A. The Nature of the University. The accusations made against this university community as a whole and would seek to understanding of the methods and functions of administrators, faculty, and staff in a university. There is a failure to comprehend that faculty are an integral part of a university and, as such, are found assisting in decision-making on all levels.

The charges made against KSU are not merely directed against the university community as a whole and would seek to deny not only faculty input but would also deny the modern concept prevalent in the most prestigious universities of treating college students as mature young adults instead of children and that the old concept of *in loco parentis* is not suitable in today's value system.

The university in a free society must remain as a symbol of freedom with the administration providing the setting for divergent viewpoints. Such attempts to discredit a university administration, faculty, and students by any group under color of law can only represent an attack on the very foundation of a free society. As President White has said, the attitudes expressed in the Grand Jury Report are indicative of "a brewing national disaster." The university is a community of scholars who must have freedom from undue external control in order to seek truth.

B. Freedom of Speech. The right to be heard and to hear all sides of an issue is fundamental to education and to a free society. The courts of our land have safeguarded the constitutional right to freedom of speech and have consistently ruled that speakers will not be banned from our universities merely because their viewpoints may be different from that of the present ruling administration. To advocate the stifling of dissent by the banning of unpopular speakers is an attack on the very foundation of education and shows a complete lack of understanding of the value of debate in a free society. The United States District Court (Case No. C70-974) has reminded the public in connection with the Grand Jury Report and the accompanying injunction by the Common Pleas Court of Portage County:

Robert M. O'Neil

The right of free speech is universally recognized as one of the most precious rights guaranteed by the First Amendment to the United States Constitution, and restraints upon its exercise are not lightly imposed. . . . It is now recognized that public demonstrations come within the protection of the First Amendment as an expression of free speech and assembly.

The university is one of the chief marketplaces of ideas that exists in a democratic nation and must therefore insist that freedom of speech and dissent is safeguarded for all.

C. Academic Freedom. Certain sections of the Grand Jury Report represent a direct threat to academic freedom, as well. The very fact that the Grand Jurors felt called upon to investigate and comment upon the activities of professors within their classrooms, activities which even the Grand Jury itself does not claim to have been illegal, has undoubtedly already had a chilling effect upon the teaching of at least some professors at Kent State University. If such attacks upon the rights of faculty members persist, they may well spell the end of Kent State as a major university, for the freedom of professors to teach as their consciences and professional competence dictate is the bedrock upon which the academic excellence of all of the best American colleges and universities has been built. The Report's repeated attacks upon the "overemphasis on dissent" once again betray a failure on the part of the Grand Jurors to understand the nature of education at the university level. One of the primary obligations of a university professor is to teach his students how to think critically even about institutions and values which the general community hold sacred. If university professors are compelled to abandon or even restrict their efforts to accomplish this end, both the universities and the nation will have suffered a great loss.

G

EXCERPTS FROM
THE REPORT OF THE
SELECT COMMITTEE

II. Faculty Rights and Obligations

   A. Findings.   1. The committee received a number of complaints that some faculty members and teaching assistants have been derelict in their responsibilities to meet instructional obligations, to provide guidance in proper conduct to students, and to maintain order. Instances were reported where faculty members had condoned or actively encouraged disruptive activities by stu-

   This interim report of the Select Committee to Investigate Campus Disturbances was presented to the 108th Ohio General Assemby pursuant to Amended Substitute Senate Concurrent Resolution 34.

dents and had even participated in such activities, had failed to teach the scheduled course content, had failed without excuse to meet scheduled classes, had made unwarranted and repeated use of obscene language in open class, and before other students had ridiculed and degraded students holding political and social opinions opposed to their own.

2. It was found that although responsible faculty members generally deplore derelictions in professional obligations by their colleagues, there is little or no enforcement of professional discipline. In part, this stems from a fear that discipline in such matters would interfere with academic freedom. The committee also found lack of uniformity in disciplinary procedures for faculty misconduct.

3. The committee received a substantial amount of testimony and evidence revealing a marked tendency to deemphasize teaching in favor of research and publication. In part, this appears due to the fact that research and publication, and not teaching, weigh most heavily in gaining professional recognition and advancement. Since teaching and counseling graduate students provide the best opportunities for research and publication, it was found that graduate students tend to monopolize a disproportionate share of many faculty members' time and that undergraduate courses, and particularly freshman and sophomore courses, tend to be left more to junior faculty members and teaching assistants.

4. A number of complaints were received concerning the quality of the instruction in certain courses, and it appeared that such complaints most often centered about junior faculty members and teaching assistants. It was found that university teachers, unlike elementary and secondary school teachers, are not required to undergo even rudimentary training in techniques, and whether or not they have any training or experience in teaching at the outset is usually a matter of chance. Further, they receive little or no supervision in their instructional duties.

5. One criticism frequently leveled at faculty members is that many do not make themselves sufficiently accessible to students for guidance and consultation. The committee found justification

for this criticism, but it also found that most faculty members conscientiously try to hold themselves available to students but that students frequently do not trouble themselves to seek out faculty members for consultation. Also, large class size sometimes makes it impossible for faculty members to give more than token individual attention to students.

6. It was noted that in many universities the employment, advancement, and discharge of faculty members has largely been assumed by department chairmen and academic deans, with little supervision being exercised from higher administrative levels. Further, the methods for monitornig the performance of faculty members are haphazard, and at many institutions apparently little or nothing is done in this regard. Classroom performance is seldom monitored. Some universities provide for student critique of faculty performance, and some do not.

7. The committee found that although in most universities tenure is granted to faculty members only after they have completed a more or less extended period of service, in some cases it is granted without any probationary period at the institution granting it. It was also suggested to the committee that tenure is used to protect a faculty member from the consequences of incompetence or misconduct.

8. It was asserted to the committee that some research projects are undertaken by the universities, which projects are either unrelated to the educational function or hinder its performance in some degree. In this connection, it was stated that in many cases time spent on research by faculty members is time which would do greater service if spent in teaching. At one university, it was revealed that nearly one-third of the total complement of faculty members do not teach because their full time is occupied in research.

B. Recommendations. 1. The committee recommends the adoption of a code of minimum standards of professional conduct and discipline. Like the code of student conduct and discipline recommended in this report, such code might be adopted by direct legislative action, or the Board of Regents might be required to promulgate such a code, or universities might be required to submit proposed codes to the Board of Regents for final approval for purposes of standardization.

Such code should set forth the obligations of faculty members to their schools, with particular reference to their instructional obligations and also to their duties to provide students with guidance in proper standards of conduct, and to maintain order. The code should define academic freedom and state with some particularity the rights and responsibilities embraced by the concept. Such code should also reflect the fact that the personal behavior of faculty members cannot entirely be disassociated from their professional lives. The code should provide appropriate sanctions for professional and personal misconduct, together with guidelines for imposing such sanctions.

Adequate provision should be made in such code to insure that faculty members accused of misconduct have reasonable notice of the charges against them, are afforded a fair opportunity to defend themselves before an impartial board or officer, and that one administrative review is available to determine the regularity of the proceedings and the sanctions imposed. Provision should be made for the privacy of the proceedings at the accused's request. The code of faculty conduct and discipline should provide that whether an offender is tenured or not is irrelevant to the imposition of appropriate sanctions for misconduct.

2. The committee recommends that tenure not be granted to a faculty member until he has demonstrated his competence and suitability during a probationary period at such institution. In the case of an experienced faculty member coming from another institution, the probationary period should not be less than one academic year, with longer minimum periods specified in other cases.

3. The committee recommends that at least some instruction in teaching techniques or experience in teaching should be required to qualify prospective faculty members and teaching assistants for their positions. Senior faculty members charged with supervising junior faculty members and teaching assistants should take appropriate measures to monitor and evaluate the performance of those

under their supervision and to insure that they acquire increasing competence as teachers.

3. The committee recommends that at least some instruction in teaching techniques or experience in teaching should be required to qualify prospective faculty members and teaching assistants for their positions. Senior faculty members charged with supervising junior faculty members and teaching assistants should take appropriate measures to monitor and evaluate the performance of those under their supervision and to insure that they acquire increasing competence as teachers.

4. The committee recommends that universities immediately evaluate the effectiveness of their respective policies, methods, and procedures in regard to the accessibility to students of not only faculty members but administrators at all levels for guidance and consultation. Every effort should be made to maintain a high level of personal contact and to provide students with as much personal attention as possible. In this regard, the committee reminds administrators and faculty members that it considers undergraduate programs to be of primary importance to any university and suggests that senior faculty members should give increased attention to such programs and should give particular attention to freshmen and sophomores, who in the committee's opinion are often those most in need of mature guidance and counseling. Further, the committee suggests that universities should emphasize their instructional functions and consider research functions as important but clearly secondary.

5. The committee recommends that additional study be given to the employment, advancement, performance, and discharge of faculty members, with a view to determining the best methods of insuring that adequate supervision is exercised in such matters, that teaching performance is given due recognition, and that faculty members have at the outset, and maintain, a high level of competence. In this connection, also, the alternatives for monitoring faculty performance should be examined.

6. The committee recommends that further study be given to research projects being carried on by the universities with par-

ticular attention to: the origins of such projects; how such projects relate to the main mission of the university; the number of faculty members engaged in such projects; and the extent to which research projects may unduly limit the availability of faculty for teaching duties. . . .

VI. Conclusion

In its interim report, the committee has stated that further study is needed, at least in the following areas: the nature of legislation needed to insure that financial assistance is not wasted on students guilty of serious misconduct (Recommendation 1-B-2); the employment, advancement, performance, and dismissal of faculty (Recommendation 11-B-5); the conflict between teaching and research (Recommendation 11-B-6); questions related to the future directions of higher education in Ohio (Recommendation 111-B-1); dormitory financing (Recommendation 111-B-5); the awarding of grades and course credits for incomplete work and the refund of fees when campuses are closed due to disorder (Recommendation 111-B-7); and evidence of a conspiracy to disrupt higher education (Recommendation V-B).

The committee has further stated, with respect to those campus problems which ought to be solved by the academic communities themselves, but which are not or cannot be solved by them, that legislative solutions will be necessary.

In addition to the issues discussed in this interim report, there are other matters which have been before the committee and to which the committee will be giving further consideration.

Accordingly, the committee will continue its work and in this connection will visit the campuses of the state universities, first, to pursue those inquiries concerning which further study is needed, and, second, to consult with administrators, faculty members, and students on what progress has been and is being made by the academic communities in resolving their own problems. In addition, the committee intends to acquire immediate and first-hand knowledge with respect to any campus disorder which may occur. If in the course of its continuing inquiries the committee determines that legislation is urgently needed to correct any problems or prevent disorder and prosecute offenders, it will request the Governor to call a special session forthwith.

H

HINDS COUNTY
GRAND JURY REPORT

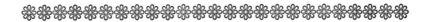

The Highway Patrol came to the campus of Jackson State College on the nights of May 13th and 14th to assist the Jackson Police Department, who had found themselves unable to handle the bad situation without help. The Jackson Police were in charge and the Highway Patrol took all their orders and instructions from the officer in command of the Jackson Police Department at all times.

Every member of the Mississippi Highway Patrol who was present at Jackson State College understood that commands would be taken from the officer in charge of the Jackson Police Department on the scene. The Mississippi Highway Patrolmen followed

The grand jury report on the Jackson State disorders, excerpted here, appeared on July 29, 1970.

these commands and instructions to the letter. There was never a time when a single policeman or patrolman violated any command.

It was most unfortunate that the Mayor of the City of Jackson saw fit to appear on television and make statements to the press to the effect that the Jackson Police Department officers did not fire their weapons at Jackson State College. This statement was absolutely false and the Mayor in making it has brought extreme and unwarranted criticism upon the Mississippi Highway Patrol and its officers. This action of the Mayor, in the opinion of this Grand Jury, is reprehensible and should not be excused or cannot be justified.

The Mayor of the City of Jackson testified before this Grand Jury that in his opinion the best qualified man in the entire Jackson Police Department capable of exercising the responsibility of command in a riot or civil disorder situation was on May 13, 14, and 15, 1970, out of the state attending a special training school. Consequently, the City of Jackson Police Department, in the opinion of the Mayor of the City of Jackson, was without the best qualified officer capable of exercising command in a riot or civil disorder.

It was, therefore, necessary on both May 13th and 14th for the Police Department to place in command of the Jackson Police Department detachment in the Jackson State College riot a Lieutenant of Police. This Police Lieutenant was required to obtain his orders in every communication with the Mayor.

This Police Lieutenant on May 14th on at least three occasions immediately prior to the unfortunate incidents in which two persons were killed and others wounded requested authority by radio from the Assistant Chief of Police for permission to use tear gas.

These requests were made by the Police Lieutenant in the immediate area of Stewart Hall on Lynch Street. The Assistant Chief of Police relayed this request to the Mayor of the City of Jackson. The Mayor stated that he delayed a decision on the use of gas until the Guard had moved into the area.

The Mayor of the City of Jackson was near the scene of the disorders at Jackson State College on both May 13th and 14th giving directions and advice to the police. As a matter of fact, the police were hesitant to act without first receiving the expressed authority to do so. . . .

In the future, the handling of riots or civil disorders should be left to the trained and experienced police at the site on whose judgment we must rely.

The senior officers of both the Mississippi Highway Patrol and the Jackson Police Department who were at the scene feel that had they been permitted to use tear gas when requested, the riot would have promptly ended and, in all probability, the situation at Alexander Hall would not have occurred. We concur in this opinion.

This Grand Jury heard direct testimony from members of the Jackson Police Deparmtent that they fired their riot control shotguns a number of times in this instance. These officers and others further testified that prior to the hearings before the Mayor's Lawyers and Committee or Ad Hoc Forum which began on May 16th that all of the officers of the Jackson Police Department who were actually present in the Jackson Police Department detail on Lynch Street in front of Alexander Hall at about midnight on May 14th were called into a meeting at the Police Department presided over by a Deputy Chief of Police and the Director of Personnel.

The Deputy Chief of Police informed these men that each of them would be expected to appear before this committee that the Mayor had appointed and make statements. They were told that if they did not do so that they would suffer the consequences.

It was made clear to these twenty-two men by this Deputy Chief of Police that they faced disciplinary action and dismissal if they did not cooperate, and they were required to put their name on a yellow pad to indicate they would make the required statements.

The lieutenant was told by the Deputy Chief to take the names of those officers who would not cooperate by making a statement, indicating to the Lieutenant disciplinary action against the men was intended. These officers were extremely reluctant to appear before this committee because they believed it would be composed of at least three members who were already publicly opposed to anything that law enforcement, and particularly Jackson police, stood for.

This Grand Jury believes that these twenty-two officers were subjected to the rankest kind of pressure and intimidation by the Mayor, his committee and this Deputy Chief of Police. We feel strongly that insofar as investigations or other actions concerning statements that any of these twenty-two officers might have previously given be brought to an end with this Grand Jury report.

We wish to make it clear that any further action of any kind against any of the twenty-two police officers inovlved by the Mayor of the City of Jackson or the Police Department of the City of Jackson would be unwarranted, unjustified, and political in nature.

There were forty-two members of the Mississippi Highway Patrol involved in the Jackson State College riot and disorder.

This Grand Jury is the only body that has the power and authority to investigate acts such as occurred at Jackson State College on May 13th and May 14th. The committee appointed by the Mayor was nothing more than an illegal and unlawful civilian review board. We do not feel that this kind of committee can ever be expected to act in the best interest of or benefit the public and the State of Mississippi.

The Mayor's Committee, or at least three members of it, in this situation drew unwarranted and unfounded conclusions on inaccurate, incomplete, and insufficient statements. It is most unfortunate for the City of Jackson that this committee was ever appointed.

The President of Jackson State College advised this Grand Jury that on May 14th he requested that Lynch Street be closed off in the Jackson State College area in order to avoid further difficulty. He contacted the Assistant Chief of Police for the City of Jackson and specifically requested that Lynch Street be closed in the Jackson State College area stating his reasons for said request. The Assistant Chief of Police replied that he did not have the authority to close the street; that this was a decision that would have to be made by the Mayor of the City of Jackson who at the time was unavailable. . . . The President of Jackson State College stated that in his opinion the difficulties experienced on the campus of Jackson State College on the night of May 14th and early morning hours of May 15th would have probably been prevented had the City of Jackson closed Lynch Street at Jackson State College as he requested. This Grand Jury agrees.

This Grand Jury has the following recommendations:

(1) That the line of communications between the Jackson Police Department and the Jackson State College Security Police be improved. This should be done with some type of instant communications set up between the departments.

(2) This jury feels strongly that the Jackson State Security Police force should be enlarged in number. The number of officers on the present force is totally inadequate for the security job that they have to perform.

(3) This jury feels strongly that certain persons have made contradictory statements to this Grand Jury and investigative bodies. This has resulted in a failure to identify certain individuals involved in the riot and disorder at Jackson State College on May 13th, 14th, and 15th.

This Grand Jury would sincerely urge these individuals to reappraise their former statements and to come forward with the whole truth. The District Attorney stands ready to receive all statements and present them to a future grand jury.

(4) This Grand Jury strongly recommends that the flow of traffic on Lynch Street through the campus of Jackson State College should be stopped and the street closed to traffic if a feasible and workable plan be devised. This jury considers this problem to be very serious in the entire Jackson State College situation, and we earnestly request that the Zoning and Planning Boards of the City of Jackson and the appropriate agencies of the State of Mississippi promptly move in such a way that Lynch Street may be permanently closed to traffic in the Jackson State College area and that this street then could be placed under the control of Jackson State College officials and in the future that they maintain law and order.

(5) This Grand Jury strongly recommends that the Board of Institutions of Higher Learning, if necessary, exercise more direct control of campus facilities and students as well as student organizations coming under the control of the various departments of the college, and the Grand Jury feels strongly that any student, faculty member, or college personnel who participates in any campus disorder or riot in which the laws of the State of Mississippi are violated should be answerable to the president of any such college and the president of any such college should have the power, authority, and duty to promptly expel or dismiss any such student, faculty member, or college employee.

(6) This Grand Jury urgently recommends to this Court that when the next Grand Jury convenes in this judicial district that the Grand Jury be charged specifically to investigate the unrest, dissatisfaction, and multiple retirement of key and experienced senior police personnel. This Grand Jury did not have adequate time because of its other important investigations to thoroughly investigate this deplorable situation in the Police Department. . . .

The Grand Jury highly commends Major L. C. Bennett of the Police Department for the excellent manner in which felony cases from the City of Jackson were presented to this Grand Jury. We also commend M. B. Pierce, Assistant Chief of Police and Chief of Detectives of the Jackson Police Department and the Detective Bureau of the Jackson Police Department for the splendid manner in which their cases are prepared and documented. . . .

The Sheriff of Hinds County and his department are commended for its outstanding service and use of its deputies to the Grand Jury while in session. They are also commended for law enforcement within the county.

This Grand Jury greatly appreciates the assistance of the U.S. Department of Justice and the Federal Bureau of Investigation. We feel that we have had their full cooperation, and all of their investigation and information has been turned over to us for our consideration. We commend each of these agencies for their efforts in this matter.

We request the Court to direct a copy of this final report

to United States District Judge Harold Cox for his information and consideration. This Grand Jury formally requests Judge Cox to see to it that a copy of this report in its entirety is made available to the Federal Grand Jury now in session in order that they might have the benefit of our findings, in the event Judge Cox feels that this action would be appropriate.

We also request the Court to direct the Clerk to send a copy of this report to President Richard M. Nixon and his committee on campus disorders.

The Grand Jury wishes to extend thanks and appreciation to the President of Jackson State College and the faculty for their courtesies extended to this Grand Jury while visiting Jackson State College.

This Grand Jury feels that law enforcement officers should not be required or expected to testify before any local, state, or federal committee or investigative body unless they have first been formally subpoenaed and all rights and immunities extended to them that would ordinarily be extended to any other witnesses in the same circumstances.

We condemn the action of any committee or group who seeks to take statements from any law enforcement officer without first placing him under subpoena.

And now having fully completed our duties, we ask to be finally discharged.

W. S. Murphy
Grand Jury Foreman
Betty D. Everett
Grand Jury Secretary

I

STATEMENT BY
RUSSELL DAVIS

I am extremely grateful for the opportunity that has been extended to me to make this report to the people of the City of Jackson. I am well aware of the fact that my actions at the time of the trouble at Jackson State and in the aftermath of that occurrence have been criticized by some of the residents of the City of Jackson. I am, of course, reconciled to the fact that I have been and will be in the future criticized for some of the things that I do as your Mayor. I take the position that this exposure to criticism goes with the job and I have tried not to become too sensitive in this area. I want all of you to know that I feel that I did take posi-

Davis, mayor of Jackson, prepared this statement in response to the Hinds County Grand Jury report of July 31, 1970.

tive steps to give this community leadership at a time when two men had been killed and several people had been wounded. I made conciliatory statements directed to the people of this City, and I appointed a committee of five attorneys to assist me in my elected responsibility as Mayor and Police Commissioner to determine the facts in connection with the incident at Jackson State. I was in my office on the afternoon of the funeral of one of the young men who had been killed at Jackson State, and a friend told me on that occasion that he felt that I had done everything possible to calm the area of our citizens that needed to be persuaded to abandon further actions that could lead to violence; and, if no further deaths, injuries or destruction of property occurred, some of the credit would be mine. As we all know, no further violence erupted, and the City has gone forward. I sincerely hope that no further serious trouble will be forthcoming.

The Grand Jury Report as to the conclusions reached in connection with my actions, which was released on July 29, 1970, is, in my opinion, an unwarranted personal attack on your Mayor. The report as to my actions is incomplete in that it leaves out vital information, and this failure to accurately report the problems of the City Administration in the light of the existing situation is somewhat unfair to all of us. A Grand Jury is respected by our citizens as a basic part of our English common law heritage of freedom and justice. It is not my intention to criticize the Grand Jury system or the qualified freeholders of this county who were selected to serve as a part of their civic duty on this body. It is my responsibility to answer to you, the People of this City, the charges that have been made against me as your Mayor and as your Police Commissioner. It is my considered opinion that the Grand Jury was encouraged to issue this report by certain political officeholders who would like to destroy me and who do not particularly care how much damage they do to the People of the City of Jackson in the process. I want to serve notice on these people at this time that it will not be easy to destroy me. I intend to fight for the things that I believe the People of this City must have in order to enjoy a secure and a happy future. If I can accomplish this by serving in the office that you have entrusted to me in a proper manner, I believe that you the People will know what I have accomplished. The destruction of a man who does his best could prove to be somewhat difficult. There is a strong possibility that the effort to discredit me is motivated by a desire for personal political gain or to prevent needed changes in the Police Department of this City.

Our Police Department primarily consists of dedicated men, and I have always taken pride in the fact that we have so many dedicated officers in this department. For more than ten years the Chief of Police has not really been in charge of the Police Department. His resignation was requested in July of last year, and he contacted his attorney, who is also the District Attorney, and requested this man to defend him in the event his discharge was pressed. The resignation was not pressed at that time because it would have resulted in serious disruptions of the Police Department. Events that have occurred since last July have made it necessary at this time that this change be made. The Grand Jury Report makes no mention of the Chief of Police, his actions on the night of May 13, or his absence on the night of May 14.

I have this day contacted the Chief of Police and have requested in writing that he tender to me his resignation immediately. I pledge to you that I will make every effort to find and appoint a capable, qualified, experienced and dedicated man to be your Chief of Police. This man will have full authority to actually run the Police Department.

The Grand Jury Report makes several serious charges against the Major and Police Commissioner of the City of Jackson. I will try to answer these conclusions of the Grand Jury in a logical and reasonable manner. There appears to be criticism of the fact that I was on the scene and attempted to perform my duty in the office that you elected me to. I do not believe that you would have wanted me not to have been present and trying to do my job at a time when considerable turmoil was in progress in this city. The statement was made in the Grand Jury Report that my statement to the effect that the Jackson Police did not fire their weapons was reprehensible and should not be excused and could not be justified.

The Citizens of Jackson will remember that at that time I had received transcribed copies of tape recorded statements from witnesses to the incidents at Jackson State. These statements are in my office for any citizen of Jackson to read in their entirety. My effort was to preserve the good name of your Police Department and it is unfortunate that a few men have since cast shadows upon the integrity of an entire department.

The failure to use gas is laid at my feet by this report. The one instance in which I suggested that gas be delayed until the Guard had moved in, occurred when the Police and Highway Patrol were at Stewart Hall. The Guard of more than 100 men was standing at ready when I arrived at Valley and Lynch. I asked that these men be sent in. They were sent in with orders from their superiors not to put live ammunition in their guns. The crowd at Stewart Hall, that is the Men's Dormitory, was dispersed without the use of gas and it was some twenty minutes after this that the shooting occurred at Alexander Hall—this is the Women's Dormitory. No other request for gas was ever relayed to me and it is certain that Lt. McGee would have used gas prior to gunfire in any event had he given any order relative to the discharge of any weapon.

The report refers to the Committee that I appointed as "illegal and unlawful." One of our City Commissioners called on the Attorney General's office for an opinion using the same words "illegal and unlawful." The Attorney General replied to the effect that the Committee which had been appointed on an informal basis for the purpose of assisting me as Mayor and Police Commissioner with a very important investigation had been properly set up on my authority and that the City Council could dissolve the Committee if it chose to do so. The Committee before its discharge did not release or file any conclusions or findings and I believe that the Committee was legally constituted and performed a valuable and worthwhile service to this community.

Two of our most experienced and able Circuit Judges stated in reference to the Committee that I appointed, and I quote as follows: "An examination of the Report discloses that the members of the Committee you appointed acted with all due restraint and entirely impartially and dispassionately."

I am of the opinion that this Committee served the purpose of relieving tension in this City during the days immediately following Jackson State and saved us all from further violence. I am fully aware that the formation of any biracial committee is abhorrent to those who seek refuge in the past. It may very well be that this one act on my part is responsible for the vilification contained in this Grand Jury Report.

This report refers to my failure to close Lynch Street on the night of May 14th because I was not available to Assistant Chief M. B. Pierce. I was in contact with Chief Pierce all during the day of May 14th and as late as 10:30 on the night of May 14th when I went to bed prior to being awakened at approximately 11:30 when I received a report that there was trouble at Jackson State. If those who were in a position to know the situation had requested me to close the street, I would have ordered the street closed.

I agree with the Report's request that certain individuals return and come forward with the whole truth. I agree that Lynch Street should be closed through Jackson State. This matter has been under discussion in this and other administrations for a long period of time. A thorough study has been ordered by the City Council. There is a very serious problem involving rerouting traffic. I sincerely believe that the problems can be solved and I hope that this street can be closed on a basis of fair treatment to the students at the college and the traveling public within a reasonably short time.

I agree that there is unrest and dissatisfaction within the Police Department and that it is caused to a large extent by situations that have existed for a long time. Some of these have been corrected. Most of the people who have resigned have done so because of medical disabilities or the opportunity of other employment along with a generous monthly retirement income. New State Departments have made this possible in several cases. The same thing occurred in 1966 when the ABC was formed. The worst dissidents in the Police Department are those seeking even now to form a Police union that your Mayor does not think would be in line with the safety and welfare of the people of Jackson.

Our City and our Nation are undergoing most difficult times. All about us intemperate positions are being taken in a highly emotional situation. So much is this so that most of you have begun to feel that more people are spending their waking hours finding fault with their fellow men than ever before in the history of our Country. We Mayors always have had to bear the brunt of the discontented and that will ever be our lot. When I ran to serve as your chief city official, I was determined then, and I am now, to represent all of you, male or female, big or little, child or adult, black or white, rich or poor. It was my hope then and it is now to do my part in moving our City forward in all phases of our life; education, business, recreation, and to maintain peace and harmony in our community. We all realize that the preservation of order and mutual help and respect are vital.

Ever since January we have had to cope with the drastic changes in our local schools. You are all aware of the bewildering complexity of the rumors, the confusion of conflicting claims, proceedings, orders and appeals. The resultant turmoil brought on great unrest among all of our citizens. To maintain calm and to work constructively to see that our children received the education to which they were entitled strained the faith, the time, and the efforts of all of our officials. This was and will continue to be a sore and a grievous problem. Certainly, it is a time to try all of us. Extremism showed its ugly hand and many passions were aroused. Tension, tough tension did exist.

As your Mayor, I joined with everyone of good will—not to run and hide, not to throw up our hands and let George do it— but to try to work ourselves out of the situation to the best advantage possible. In this setting, the Jackson State trouble burst. All reasonable men and women were aware of the grave consequences that the early trouble on that campus on May 13th could lead to in the form of violence, of death, and destruction. I called on all of our available resources to handle this matter promptly.

To say that we found ourselves in a highly critical moment

is to put it too mildly. We were faced with the prospect of more violence, more destruction, more death, and no one knew where or when such might strike or who might be an innocent victim. The prospect called for our best judgment to see that the people's tempers were calmed and peace restored: time to cool off, to let passions weaken was necessary. Such does not take place as a result of magic or of wishful thinking.

The consensus of thought of the top business and civic leaders of this City following the appointment of this lawyer's committee was that the Mayor's action in the aftermath of Jackson State had been in the best interest of this City.

I feel that every action that I have taken prior to, during, and after the Jackson State violence has been in support of my belief and conviction that we in the City of Jackson, black and white, must pull together if we are going to make any progress. I have felt and do feel that the fewer the scars that resulted from Jackson State, the better off we all would be.

I know that all of you are well aware of the report from the Research and Development Center that shows the City of Jackson to be ten years behind a proper projected schedule of progress. I want to have progress in order that we can all have a better economic future in a safe, clean, well-run and dynamic community of which we can all be justifiably proud. The only way that this can be done is by recognizing the fact that 60 per cent of our people are white and 40 per cent of our people are black and that it is to the best interest of 100 per cent of these people that they work together and that the many problems we now face may be resolved. This cannot be done immediately and we face many long months and years of hard work, sweat, and tears. Thank you very much for having given me the opportunity to talk to you tonight.

J

CHARGE OF
JUDGE COX TO THE
MISSISSIPPI GRAND JURY

Remember that you are here only to investigate federal crimes; that is, crimes for violating federal laws only. In your consideration of the Jackson State College incident, you will understand that nobody (black or white) has any right conferred upon him by Congress or by any section of the federal constitution to engage in a riot, or re-

On June 29, 1970, a federal grand jury was impaneled and summoned to consider primarily '(in the words of Judge Cox) "every aspect and angle of the civil disorders and riots and acts of anarchy occurring at Jackson State College . . . near midnight in May 1970." Much of the charge was routine and will not be excerpted here; the portions set forth below reflect the judge's instructions on the particular matters before the grand jury.

166

bellion, or to set fire to real, or personal property of another; or to shoot at peace officers; or to throw bricks or bottles or rocks at policemen, firemen, state highway patrolmen, or National Guardsmen sent into the area to protect property and restore law and order. Nobody participating in a riot or civil disorder or open combat with civil authorities, or failing to disperse on order of such authorities, or failing to immediately disassociate himself from such a group or gathering has any civil right to expect to avoid serious injury or even death where the disorder requires extreme measures and harsh treatment. You are further charged as a matter of law that any peace officer in the area under such circumstances has the unquestionable right to make the necessary and reasonable use of his firearms with live ammunition for his self-protection when it appears necessary and for the restoration of law and order. A peace officer subjected to the stresses and strains of a physical attack upon him and his comrades is expected to remain calm and act deliberately as a well trained peace officer should do at all times and under all circumstances, but he should not be held to the same accountability for his action under fire as would be expected and required of him under normal circumstances and conditions. This district will not provide safe sanctuary for militants or for anarchists or for revolutionaries of any race. Peace officers shall not be intimidated for the performance of their duties among such rebellious groups, and the processes of this court shall not be used to appease and placate such lawless pressure groups. These are just some salient points which you should bear in mind in your investigation and in your deliberation and in your decision as to whether or not to indict anybody. There may or may not have been any violation of a federal law by any of those students at the college on such occasion regardless of their misconduct. It may very well have been purely a state matter for handling and proper treatment. It is, however, a violation of federal law for any person to travel from one state to another with the view of inciting or participating in a riot. No peace officer has any right to unnecessarily kill anybody or to inflict excessive or unnecessary punishment upon any person, but these representatives of the public interest and the general welfare of our law abiding society should never be harassed or intimidated for their action in the necessary performance of their official duties under circumstances created by revolutionaries. What would our society be like or what would it be worth, but for the services of dedicated, well trained, and skillful men engaged in their business during the midnight hours of preserving law and order while the rest of us sleep?

INDEX

169

Index

Campus autonomy: threats to, 83–84; White on importance and vulnerability of, 129–132

Campus police and security forces, 45–46, 79, 93

Chronicle of Higher Education, 71

Communications within college and university campuses, 16–17, 86

Community and campus relations, 9–10, 92–98

Concerned Citizens of the Kent State University Community (CCC), 27–29, 109, 120

cox, h., 67; charge to federal grand jury, 166–168

D

Daily Kent Stater, 19, 28–29, 113–114

davis, r. c., 14–15, 42–43, 61, 105–106; criticized by county grand jury, 153–157; replies to criticism, 159–165

del corso, s., 48, 100

Delta State College (Mississippi), student demonstration at, 25

E

Emergency procedures on college and university campuses, 20–22

evers, c., 20, 77

F

Faculty: responsibility of, 89–92; recommendations of Ohio General Assembly Committee concerning, 145–151

"Faculty twenty-three" (Kent State University), 16–18, 62, 123, 139–140

Federal Bureau of Investigation, 72–75

ford, s., 63

frank, g., 63–64

H

Hawaii, University of, role of city police at, 87

hederman, h. h., 12

Hinds County (Mississippi) Grand Jury: excerpts from report of, 153–158; comments of Davis on, 159–165

hoover, j. e., 74

I

Injunctions as threat to campus autonomy, 84

J

Jackson, city of: relations with Jackson State College, 10–12; closing of swimming pools and schools of to resist integration, 58, 164; Chamber of Commerce of seeks to improve racial climate, 59; role of biracial investigation commission of, 58, 162–163

Jackson city police, 35, 104–105, 153–157, 161–165

Jackson *Clarion-Ledger* and *News,* 12

Jackson State College: campus police of, 45–46; faculty of, 7; faculty senate and organization of, 18; student body of, 4–5; security measures of after May 1970, 69–70

jones, l., 48

jordan, j., on conditions in Mississippi since May 1970, 59

K

kane, r., 55

kennedy, e. m., supports change in National Guard weapons policies, 87

Kent city council, passes antistudent legislation, 57–58

Kent *Record-Courier,* 11, 12

170

Index

Kent State University: administration of, 112–121, 124–128, 140–141; campus security force of, 38–39, 45; Center for Peaceful Change at, 72; dormitory room search at, 76; faculty of, 7; faculty responsibility at, 122–124, 127, 139–141; faculty senate of, 18; and federal grand jury, 68–69; and Music and Speech Building incident, 27, 41–43, 51, 67, 111–112; and security measures after May 1970, 69–70; student body of, 4–5; student conduct code at, 114–119, 124–126, 141

KIFNER, J., writes on Kent for *New York Times,* 57

Kudzu, Mississippi underground newspaper, 19

L

Law Enforcement Assistance Administration, 31

Lawrence, Kansas, vigilante activity, 85

LEONARD, J., 72

LOUGH, T., 63

Lynch Street (Jackson, Mississippi), 12, 14, 15, 31, 42, 49, 104–106, 153–156, 163; closing of recommended, 61, 155–156, 163; is closed, 59; effect of closing upon appearance of Jackson State College campus, 70

M

MC CARTHY, E., supports change in National Guard weapons policy, 87

Maryland, University of, student demonstration at, 51

Maryland National Guard during campus demonstration, 51

Miami, University of (Florida), ordered by state court to reopen after closing, 56

Miami University (Ohio), student demonstration at, 24

MICHENER, J., 68

Mississippi, University of, student demonstration at, 25

Mississippi Board of Trustees for Institutions of Higher Learning, 12, 54

Mississippi Federal Grand Jury, 67–68; charge of Cox to, 166–168

Mississippi Highway Patrol, 25, 35, 37, 140–141, 153–155; equipment and weapons of, 52

Mississippi Law Enforcement Assistance Division, effects change in weapons policy, 73

Mississippi National Guard, at Jackson State College disturbance, 41, 43, 47, 52, 73

Mississippi United Front, 59

Mississippi Valley State College, student demonstration and mass arrests at, 25, 30–31, 39, 51

MITCHELL, J., 68, 74

MORGAN, C., 60

N

National Association of State Universities and Land-Grant Colleges, 1970 annual meeting of, 64

New York University, court order for refund of tuition, 56

North Water Street (Kent, Ohio), 12

O

Ohio Board of Regents, revision of subsidy formula to cover campus closing summer 1970, 74

Ohio General Assembly: Amended

Index

Substitute House Bill 1219 concerning student disruptions, 77–78, 79; creates Select Committee to Investigate Campus Disturbances, 78–80; and Select Committee report, 145–151

Ohio Highway Patrol, 27, 29, 42; equipment and weapons of, 52

Ohio National Guard, 3, 23–24, 31, 37, 40–41, 48, 100–104; equipment and weapons of, 52; litigation involving authority of, 76

Ohio State University, student demonstration at, 24, 39

OLDS, G. A., becomes president of Kent State University, 69; institutes reforms in governance, 71–72

Orangeburg, South Carolina, killing of students at, 1

P

PEOPLES, J. A., 12, 39–40, 47–48, 49, 73, 104–106

Portage County Special Grand Jury, 57, 61–63, 72; comments of Kent State University faculty concerning, 139–144; comments of White concerning report of, 129–133; court decision concerning legality of report of, 125–128; indictments of, 63; and litigation concerning indictments and "gag" order, 64–66; report of, 123–128

President's Commission on Campus Unrest (Scranton Commission), report and views of, 26, 27, 33, 38, 45, 46, 59, 72, 81–82, 87–88, 99

Q

Queens College of the City University of New York, ordered by court to furnish special instruction in summer of 1970, 56–57

R

RACKLEY, A., trial of in New Haven, Connecticut, 34

RAINE, K., dismissed as Jackson State College faculty member after appointment, 70

Reserve Officers Training Corps (ROTC): as issue in campus disorder at Kent State and Jackson State, 32; building of burned at Kent State, 40, 43, 57, 61–62, 67, 100, 122–123; demonstration against at new site in spring 1971, 71

RHODES, J. A., 24, 37, 101

S

SATROM, L. A., 13, 25, 37, 100–103

SCHWARTZMILLER, D. L., 38

SEALE, B., trial of in New Haven, Connecticut, 34

SHIRLEY, A., comments on racial conditions and attitudes in Mississippi after May 1970, 59

SOLOMON, E., 10

Southern Regional Council report on Jackson State College student deaths, 33

State University of New York at Buffalo injunction against campus disorder, 84

STONE, I. F., 68

Students for a Democratic Society (SDS), 27, 67

Surveillance on college campuses, 74–75, 97

T

TAFT, R. A., JR., defeats J. Rhodes for Republican nomination for United States Senate, 25

172

Index

173